Forgetting and Forgotten:

Dementia and the Right to Die

W. Lee Hansen

LITTLE CREEK PRESS
AND BOOK DESIGN
MINERAL POINT, WISCONSIN

Little Creek Press.
5341 Sunny Ridge Road
Mineral Point, WI 53565

ORDERING INFORMATION
Quantity sales. Special discounts are available on quantity purchases by corporations, associations, and others. For details, contact info@littlecreekpress.com

Orders by US trade bookstores and wholesalers.
Please contact Little Creek Press or Ingram for details.

Printed in the United States of America

Cataloging-in-Publication Data
Names: Hansen, W. Lee, author.
Title: Forgetting and Forgotten / W. Lee Hansen
Description: Mineral Point, WI: Little Creek Press, 2023.
Identifiers: LCCN: 2023907694 | ISBN: 978-1-955656-55-9
Subjects: LAW082000 LAW / Right to Die

Book design by Little Creek Press

Background cover photo: Shutterstock

"To the millions of caregivers
who every day help family members,
friends, and patients cope with the
devastating effects of dementia."

TABLE OF CONTENTS

PREFACE

THIS BOOK HAS A curious history. It began to take shape after my wife Sally was institutionalized more than halfway through her decade-long siege of subcortical vascular dementia. Here is how it evolved.

I was struck at the time by the gap in communication between assisted living/memory care staff and the families of residents. Believing that better communications could inform, improve, and increase the interaction between staff and residents, I wrote a paper suggesting ways to facilitate this. The paper I produced reflected my long-time interest in the Deming "quality improvement" movement that flourished in the late 1980s and 1990s.

My interest then turned to understanding the risks and benefits of the antipsychotic medication Seroquel, prescribed to decrease Sally's anxiety and agitation. I was struck by the lack of attention given in federal Food and Drug Administration warnings to the benefits of Seroquel and the discounting of those benefits by medical staff.

As Sally's institutional care intensified, I became concerned about the costs of caring for people suffering from dementia. This concern led me to pull together the costs of her care, including Medicare, health insurance, hospital and home health care costs, my out-of-pocket costs, and the subsidies provided through Hospice Care. I could not help but be impressed by the high costs of maintaining elders suffering from dementia, and the obvious fact that many families are unable to access the level of care Sally received.

By this time, well into Sally's first full year of institutional care, I became preoccupied with the kind and quality of the care she was receiving. I had already begun writing memos to myself describing my almost daily visits with Sally and the care she was receiving. This record enhanced my interactions with the memory care staff and helped me observe the pattern of her decline. By the time Sally passed away, I had a detailed chronology of her deteriorating memory as well as details on the care she received.

I thought that this mass of information might provide the basis for a book manuscript about our journey through dementia, but several friends told me that few readers would be interested in the documentary records I had assembled. Readers instead would want to know the "story" of Sally's decline, my involvement in her care, and how we handled the separation we experienced as her memory worsened and her aberrant behavior increased. I suddenly realized that I had been continuing the data-driven writing approach that facilitated my career as a widely published professional economist.

In other words, friends told me I needed to tell an actual story recounting my beloved wife's decline into the darkness of dementia, including her frequent, heart-rending cries of "Help me. Help me. I am dying. I want to die. Please help me." I realized that this was the story that needed to be told. So I began writing in earnest *Forgetting and Forgotten: Dementia and the Right to Die.*

Sally's story is about a woman who long believed all individuals should have the right to die on their own terms; Sally's behavior during the last three years of her life reflected this interest. In short, Sally believed that well before a person's dementia became apparent, every individual should have the right to specify how and at what stage in their decline they wanted to die. They should be able to do so in the knowledge that their wishes would be faithfully honored by their families and by health care professionals who would be needed to assist in bringing about the person's death.

Existing legislation, whatever its name, "Assisted Suicide," "Death with Dignity," or "Medical Aid in Dying," prevents the provision of medical assistance in dying to people with dementia like Sally. Eligibility criteria require that individuals be of sound mind and already determined by a medical professional to be "terminal," meaning they can be expected to die within the coming six months. Given that people with advanced or even mild dementia cannot be described as being of sound mind, and it is impossible to determine with certainty how soon they will die, they are denied access to this relief to their suffering.

Sally's constant cries to me, "Help me, help me. I am dying. I want to die. Please help me" were heart-breaking. What could I do? Nothing. Any action I might take to assist in her death would make me liable for legal action and could well lead to local newspaper headlines: "Retired Professor Accused of Murdering Demented Wife."

So, there we were, stuck with the prospect that Sally would have to live out the rest of her pain-filled, now much-diminished existence until she died of natural causes. Sally's situation was hardly unique. Every year more than 100,000 elderly people afflicted with dementia die, many of them like Sally having lived into the stage of advanced dementia, lacking cognition, experiencing serious illnesses, and requiring extensive care by family members as well as costly home and institutional care. During this time they exist in limbo, mostly incoherent and unable to relate to family and caregivers. Survey data about the attitudes of seniors indicate that most express the wish for a quick, painless, and peaceful death. I believe that many who suffer from dementia would, if they could, invoke what they regard as their God-given Right to Die.

Books always take longer to write than their authors expect. Their authors have other responsibilities, interests, and concerns that also require their attention. Most caregivers do not view themselves as professional writers and find telling their stories more difficult than they expected.

And so it has been in my case. I continued my professional research and writing while caring for Sally at home, and I was able to continue doing so but at a slower pace while Sally was institutionalized. Since Sally passed away, I have devoted much of my time to writing this book, a memoir describing our often lonely journey through the ups and downs of dementia.

Writing this book has been both difficult and gratifying. While reliving our experience has often brought tears to my eyes, I believe that detailing how we coped offers lessons to others in similar circumstances, lessons that are found in Chapter 15: The Tool Box.

My hope is that many of the lessons I learned will benefit other caregivers. I hope that more and more states adopt "Medical Aid in Dying" legislation. I also hope that such legislation can be a prelude to Right to Die legislation of the kind Sally advocated for, legislation enabling people suffering from dementia and other fatal diseases to specify in advance when, where, and how they want to die when they are no longer capable of making such decisions for themselves, and thus break free of the heartbreaking "no exit" situation in which these sufferers are denied Death with Dignity.

W. Lee Hansen
Madison Wisconsin
January 2023

Part I

A Life Well Lived

"Remember" by Christina Rossetti

Remember me when I am gone away,
Gone far away into the silent land;
When you can no more hold me by the hand,
Nor I half turn to go yet turning stay.
Remember me when no more day by day
You tell me of our future that you planned.
Only remember me, you understand
It will be late to counsel then or pray.
Yet if you should forget me for a while
And afterwards remember, do not grieve
For if the darkness and corruption leave
A vestige of the thoughts that once I had,
Better by far you should forget and smile
Than that you should remember and be sad.

Chapter 1

THE INEVITABILITY OF DEMENTIA

Premonitions

My wife, Sally, had long believed people should have the right to determine when and how they would die. Her idea went like this: Older adults, between the ages of fifty and sixty-five, should consider the possibility that they might later suffer from dementia. To protect their right to die, individuals could make out a Dementia Right-to-Die Directive and attach it to their Advanced Medical Directive. This document would specify at what stage in their journey with dementia they wanted to have their lives terminated. The alternative, Sally believed, would be to continue living the "nonlife" of an individual suffering from dementia—that progressive, irreversible, and dreaded disease.

She and I agreed we would not want to continue living while suffering through the worst stages of dementia—when we might no longer know who we were, or even who we *had been*. We wanted to be able to exercise our right to die.

Early Thoughts

Sally's views on death and dying had begun to take shape following the death of her parents when she was still in her early thirties. Witnessing how her parents died—her mother at age sixty-five from terminal stomach cancer and her father at age seventy from congestive heart failure—stimulated her thinking. Both parents spent their last months in agony. Sally's mother, who was being cared for at the home of Sally's sister Nancy in northern California, had opted to discontinue her chemotherapy. She had the good fortune to be cared for by a collaborative nurse willing to administer ever-stronger doses of morphine. I suspected these injections eased her pain and hastened her death. Sally's father, being hospitalized after a severe stroke, was not so lucky. The hospital staff seemed more concerned with extending his life even though his prospects for any kind of successful recovery were dim. He died several weeks later rather than more quickly as he would have preferred.

Sally wondered why her parents had to suffer as they did. The answer? The medical profession's goal then was to extend life without particular regard for a patient's quality of life. More enlightened views on death and dying had not yet taken shape.

My eighty-two-year-old father's death from congestive heart failure in 1972 was, on the other hand, handled very well. The family doctor, rather than pushing for his hospitalization, urged that he remain at home and be made as comfortable as possible. The doctor recognized that my father did not have long to live and prescribed pain-reducing medication. He wanted to spare my mother the trauma that she might have experienced if my dad was hospitalized. My dad died a peaceful death several days later. This family doctor proved to be wiser than the medical specialists.

By contrast, my ninety-six-year-old mother's death twenty years later raised many questions. While living in a retirement home, she fell and broke a hip. She was given a hip replacement even though it was clear she lacked the body strength to perform the necessary rehab exercises. She languished for another three months in a nursing home, unable to do anything and experiencing considerable pain and discomfort. For whatever reason, little was done to deal with her distress. My guess is that today a hip replacement for a woman of her age would never be allowed.

For the most part, these were not easy deaths.

No Hint of What Was to Come

The death of our parents caused both Sally and I to begin to contemplate death and end-of-life issues, and some of this discussion centered on dementia, for Sally held strong views on the subject. How ironic that at this point in time, neither Sally nor I had any inkling she herself would ever experience dementia. There was no history of dementia in her family, and what I found especially peculiar was that over her lifetime, she had followed the now-current advice about how to best avoid dementia and Alzheimer's disease. She exercised regularly. She remained intellectually engaged. She interacted with her numerous friends. She ate healthy foods. She always got adequate rest.

Even when she was actively engaged in advocating for the rights of the dying, we never guessed that she would fall victim to this dread condition. Over the years, Sally did have some underlying health problems, among them periodic bouts of depression, but none of them appeared to contribute to her dementia.

Recounting Sally's life before she was overtaken by this condition and in the years that followed, I have no trouble describing the many activities she so enjoyed that were taken from her. They included visiting and interacting with her children and grandchildren, socializing with her women friends at the nearby Starbucks coffee shop, engaging with her English as a Second Language conversational partners, playing Scrabble with family members, completing the reading for her book group, and keeping up with the daily newspapers—to name just a few. Recently finding the score sheets of our Scrabble games, I was reminded how formidable a player she had been. However, at a certain point, she could no longer construct words with her Scrabble tiles.

Sally's Worsening Condition Prompts a Change in Our Lifestyle

After witnessing years of Sally's slow decline, her diminished engagement in the activities just mentioned, her growing reliance on me for her social interaction, and her increasing memory loss, it became clear that we needed to move her into the retirement home we had already selected for ourselves. An even more important reason for moving was the increased frequency of her falling; her injuries had already necessitated several visits to the local hospital's emergency room. I was looking forward to the relaxed setting of an independent-living apartment, with its adjacent assisted-living unit that would provide easy access to its memory-care community.

Sally's memory loss had initially come to my attention in early 2006. A vigorous and intellectually alive seventy-seven-year-old began to miss scheduled coffee get-togethers with friends. She became increasingly confused about her day's schedule. Sometimes she had difficulty navigating herself to the movies she wanted to see. At times she had to return to the house and ask me how to get to where she wanted to go. At first I was not certain what was happening to her, except that she was getting older, like me, and more forgetful. Finally, I realized what my eyes were beginning to see. I was losing Sally to dementia.

How did I react? Being an optimist, my approach to life's difficulties calls for finding a positive way of dealing with them rather than letting them overwhelm me. I had already coped with Sally's periodic episodes of depression when I'd had to take over management of the household and family. What proved to be most difficult was my inability to converse with her—we'd always had such good conversations with each other. I also began reading books and reports on dementia and caregiving, and this proved to be a major help.

In the spring of 2008, a visit to Sally's psychiatrist led him to schedule a memory test for her. After the results of that testing were completed by the Wisconsin Institute for Research on Alzheimer's Disease, we met with its director and the staff social worker. The doctor explained that Sally suffered from mild cognitive loss. Not only that, she was also diagnosed with subcortical vascular dementia. The explanation? As I detail later in the book, she had suffered a series of small strokes in her brain that had caused some memory loss.

Many people are unclear of the difference between Alzheimer's disease and dementia and how they relate to one another. Alzheimer's is a form of dementia and is the most prevalent form found today, followed by vascular dementia of which subcortical vascular dementia is one type. (Please see tool 4, in the Tool Box of this book, found in chapter 13, for more on the different types of dementia.)

Any type of vascular dementia may result in reduced oxygen and nutrients reaching the cells of the brain. As a result, brain cell death occurs, causing confused thinking, memory issues, and reasoning abilities. The sum total of these symptoms is defined as cognition. All too frequently, these symptoms manifest and worsen. This, in turn, affects the afflicted individual's quality of life. As a result, a diagnosis of vascular dementia—which is diagnosed based on the symptoms alone since a test for it does not exist—may ensue.

Like vascular dementia, Alzheimer's disease is a result of the death of brain cells, and in this case as a result of plaques in the brain that are made up of atypical proteins. Many of the symptoms are the same as those of vascular dementia, and like vascular dementia, there is no test for Alzheimer's. Typically, a definitive diagnosis is made by way of a brain autopsy only after the individual has passed on. There is no cure at present for Alzheimer's disease.

In Sally's case, when the doctor told her that she had mild cognitive loss and subcortical vascular dementia, she knew enough to ask, "Did you find any evidence of Alzheimer's disease?" The psychiatrist said he had not, adding that at her age she was unlikely to ever suffer from that particular form of dementia. Though obviously relieved, Sally asked for more information on her life chances. The doctor indicated that over time her dementia would worsen and eventually she would succumb to it. He wanted her to come back in a year so he could check its progress.

Sally's Outward Reaction

Sally received this jarring news rather calmly. I sensed she knew what was happening to her—dementia was taking hold of her. She must have been terrified. What can be worse than a sense that you are losing your self, your memories, your mental capacities, and all that go with them? Her inner world must have felt disjointed and terrifying. Mine did, too. But knowing she suffered in silence was also part of my pain. I never knew for sure what she knew and didn't know as she began to lose her memory—and so much more.

I worried constantly that something dangerous and frightening was happening to my lovely Sally. For me, this was the start of the conflictive and paradoxical nature of knowing what was happening to a loved one when they are losing their memory and other faculties that had always been part of their identity.

Unknowns and Uncertainties

From that point on, everything shifted. I became painfully aware that the golden years we had expected to spend together—traveling, visiting grandchildren, taking up new hobbies, catching up on our reading—were no longer possible. Sally would take a fear-filled decline into the darkness of dementia. As her husband and caregiver, I would take a journey into my own darkness.

Every day brought a host of unknowns—strange visitors like ghosts, haunting everything we did. They were unknowns that I would face without Sally's intelligence, wit, independence, and generosity, which had been her nature for the more than fifty years we had lived together. Life became like living in a poorly lit room, and I had no idea where to find the light switch. My ongoing job was to find the light switch and lead us into the next room where just maybe there would be more light, more answers, and more hope.

There are so many unknowns that arrive at one's doorstep when dementia becomes a central focus of life. For the elderly facing dementia, not knowing how their dementia will unfold haunts them. When I asked Sally why she was not going as regularly to her warm-water pool exercise class, she told me she was embarrassed by her inability to remember the names of her pool mates. She said much the same when I asked her about attending Sunday services at the Unitarian Meeting House. She also wondered how she could relate to our daughters and grandchildren when she could no longer remember what they had just talked about. Sally soon became aware of how her dementia would change her from the person she had always been to some less complete person whose memory was failing, whose interests in life were diminishing, and whose physical condition was deteriorating.

The biggest unknown was how long Sally would continue to live in her demented state. Nobody could say. What a frightening possibility. Might a new scientific breakthrough throw light on the causes of dementia and lead to some way of reversing its inevitable progress? No breakthroughs seemed to be on the horizon, even as research on dementia and particularly on

Alzheimer's disease accelerated. No medications were available that could effectively slow her decline.

Again, as a caregiver and husband, I faced my own set of unknowns. How long would Sally continue living with her increased memory loss and dementia? How rapidly was she likely to decline as her memory faded and she required even more care? How would her behavior change as dementia tightened its grip on her? How would I be able to experience the slow loss of someone with dementia who was there but not really with me? These questions tore at me because there were no answers.

In addition to the unknowns were the uncertainties. How rapidly would Sally's dementia pass from its mild stage to its more severe stages? Is it likely that Sally would have to be institutionalized to ensure her proper care? An overarching uncertainty was whether I could deal with these fearful prospects. Our daughters realized that the mother they knew no longer recognized them, and there was little they could do about that.

These unknowns and uncertainties are the mental baggage we loved ones carry around in our brains and memories, waiting for some relief. But in the case of dementia, relief never comes. Even the simple joys of one's day are often forgotten or eclipsed by the constant attention we give to those we care for.

Unpredictables

On top of the unknowns and the uncertainties there are the unpredictables. These are the often perplexing and unexpected changes in our loved one's behavior that can occur over short periods of time—from day to day and often from hour to hour. I had heard other caregivers talk about such changes. These behavioral changes proved to be far more difficult for me to deal with than any of the larger unknowns.

At times, and for unexplained reasons, Sally would throw dishes at the staff at the care facility, drop a cup of coffee on the floor, or take food from the plates of other residents. I cringed when I heard about these behaviors. I cringed for her and for myself.

It's analogous to a situation wherein your adult child who has done so well in life takes a sudden and drastically different turn for the worse.

Relatives ask how your adult child is doing and you find ways to change the subject or just nod and mention some reasonable cliché that will stop the questions. I cringed at my own cringing. We don't want to feel this way about someone we love, but the one we love is disappearing before our very eyes.

I soon encountered what I call the "caregiver's plight." How could I best adapt to Sally's decline as dementia took ever-increasing control of her brain and altered her behavior? What could I do to ensure she received the care that would best maintain her quality of life? In thinking along these lines, I realized I was pulling away from my immediate concerns with Sally's behavior to think about the bigger issues I faced, especially after she had to be moved to memory care. After that, these issues would seem more manageable. The facility's trained memory-care staff could deal with Sally's often strange behaviors—whatever they were.

My challenge was to work with the staff and particularly the wellness nurses so that they did their best for Sally. This called for me to indicate my concerns to them in order to best draw upon their training, experience, and advice. Once I did this, life became easier for me. I quickly learned where to put my focus and energy. Once my role was better defined, I experienced some relief.

I continued visiting Sally regularly, to talk with her, to reassure her, and to indicate my undying support for her despite her dementia-induced confusion. In truth, I had to distance myself from her to maintain my own equilibrium. This was not an easy thing to do but was something that was essential. Though there was nothing I could do to respond to her request that I help her die, I could try to help her when she voiced complaints about her life.

Though all this may sound a bit muddled, perhaps it was. That is part of what it means to be a caregiver.

Our Marriage

How did Sally's dementia affect our marriage? Sally and I had always viewed our marriage as a highly successful one. We believed that from our first encounters we were well matched. Throughout our marriage, we had little conflict. Although our views on many issues differed, our respect for each other overcame any minor disagreements. I always thought of our marriage as one of those "till death do us part" arrangements.

As Sally slipped into dementia, our love for each other evolved. Sally regularly professed her love for me, and I did the same to her. My obligation was to ensure that Sally continued to receive the best care possible. This often proved to be difficult to achieve because she was no longer the person she had once been. As a result, I had to display great patience and compassion in my dealings with her. Fortunately, I was blessed with enough resilience to manage it all.

Our premonition of wanting to secure a legal right-to-die option even when dementia was a reality was always haunting me. This became particularly apparent in the last fifteen months of Sally's life when she regularly said, "Help me. Help me. I'm dying. I want to die," as she sought my assistance in doing so. Having advocated for the right to die for others when she was a younger woman, she was now advocating for the right to die herself. Unfortunately, however, there was nothing I or anyone else could do to help her. Our two daughters knew their mother's wishes, having heard her say that when she was no longer the person she once was, the plug should be pulled. But of course, there was no plug to pull, meaning no legal way to implement her wish.

But there was another big question. Before Sally died, would the time come when her asserted right to die could be honored? This is the larger issue that pervades this book.

Individuals who fear they may become demented should be able to instruct their caregivers long beforehand on when and how they want to die and have these instructions carried out, rather than living out their demented lives until they die of natural causes. Yes, I believe Sally's desire to die was genuine, and if it had been legal for me to do so, I would have honored her wish.

My decade-long journey with Sally into and through the strange, baffling world of dementia is remembered here. I find this ironic. Here I am writing about my beloved wife's loss of memory, relying on my own memory to recall the story. In this recounting, I am also advocating as best I can for other elderly caregivers who want their loved ones to live and die with dignity and who want their loved ones with dementia to have the right to choose how and when to depart from this world.

But when do we make this choice? Once Sally became aware of her dementia, she did not want me to even mention the word (although she soon relented). Do we live in a culture that denies death, one where people don't want to think about it or even mention it because of the discomfort it brings us? As a result, we don't hold the difficult but important conversations early on in our lives. These are dialogues that will clear the way for more direct and meaningful discussions as the end of life approaches. Fortunately, more help in conducting these discussions is available today than ever before.

My journey with Sally gives attention to the final three years of her life in an assisted living/memory-care facility and her end-of-life care. Her journey into the darker stages of dementia and beyond started with her being moved into a memory-care community.

Chapter 2

OUR EARLY LIFE

MY FIRST ENCOUNTER WITH Sally Porch in the summer of 1954 was a strange one. As a house fellow in the Lakeshore dorms at the University of Wisconsin-Madison, I arrived early for the house fellow orientation before the summer school students arrived. When Sally, another house fellow, reached her dorm late in the afternoon after an all-day train trip from Detroit, she needed a key to her room. Paul Ginsberg, the head house fellow, invited me to go with him to deliver the key. Paul introduced us and gave Sally her key. Then he asked if we could carry her two heavy suitcases to her third-floor room. She responded dismissively, "I can manage that myself." I was startled by her response. Most young women would have gladly accepted such an offer. With that, Sally picked up her two bags and briskly headed up the stairs. Paul later remarked that Sally was quite obviously a very independent woman.

So began the summer of 1954, when as graduate students we both served as house fellows in the Lakeshore dormitories. Unlike so many summer school students, we focused on our academic work.

Sally had spent the 1952–53 academic year at Madison taking graduate courses in the English Department. She came back in the summer of 1954 to prepare for her master's degree examination in English literature at the end of the summer.

After almost three years of military service during the Korean War, I began my graduate work at Madison in the spring semester of 1954. That summer, I enrolled in two courses required for my master's degree in economics. At the same time, I was completing work on what would become my first published research paper.

Sally concentrated on preparing for her exam, planning to return to Dearborn, Michigan, during the fall semester to continue her career as a high school English teacher. As the summer months passed, I came to know her fairly well when a group of house fellows, ourselves included, convened frequently in the Pine Room of the dorm, sitting at a large table, drinking coffee and conversing. Sally impressed me with her intellect, lively personality, independence, and feminist inclinations, as well as her tendency to speak her mind, often in a quite dramatic fashion.

At one memorable weekly house fellow meeting to decide whether to continue each dorm's subscription to the Sunday edition of *The New York Times*, she recommended stopping the subscriptions. She reported that her dorm residents never read the paper, or as she put it, the newspaper was "untouched by human hands!" Not surprisingly, this comment provoked much laughter, proved to be decisive, and the Sunday *New York Times* was no more.

Sally the Feminist

As the summer progressed, I learned that Sally was an early feminist intent on making her own way in the world. She talked about forgoing marriage for a teaching career, inspired by an admired maiden aunt who held a doctoral degree and taught at a California college, traveled widely, and lived a happy, satisfying life. Sally mentioned her plan for the next summer: to head for Europe "to work on a post-war reconstruction project." She didn't strike me as quite the type but I did not say anything.

Although I was comfortable talking with Sally on a casual basis, she impressed me as much too formidable a woman to approach for a date. She was very serious about her studies and about life in general. Nonetheless,

I regularly kidded her about not studying hard enough for her upcoming master's degree exam scheduled for Friday, a week before the end of summer school. Sally's friends cringed when I made these remarks, knowing how serious Sally was about her academic work. She passed her exam with flying colors, which came as no surprise to me. In fact, her examining committee encouraged her to go on for a Ph.D. in English literature.

Arranging That First Date

Our serious interest in one another began with an innocent request. During the last week of summer school, Sally approached me after dinner one night with a request. "I want to help a good friend of mine, Helen, (another house fellow). I wonder if you will help me."

She continued by saying "Helen has her eye on a good friend of yours, Bob. She asked me to ask you to ask Bob to join Helen and the two of us on a double date this coming Friday night. I don't think Helen has a ghost of a chance with Bob, but I still want to help her out. So, will you ask Bob to join us?"

Sally's invitation to me came as a surprise because although Sally and I knew each other, we had not dated one another. But being a good sport, I said fine. With that, I asked Bob to join us, and he agreed. So, it was all set—a Friday night, end-of-summer-school celebration.

I looked forward to the evening, wondering whether any sparks would fly between Bob and Helen. I had no particular romantic interest in Sally, and I don't think she had any romantic interest in me. I was just trying to help out a friend, and whatever happened, I thought Sally would be an interesting date.

That fateful Friday night arrived. After dinner in the Van Hise Dining Room, Bob and I picked up the girls from their dorms. We then walked several blocks to a nearby campus hangout, a tavern called the Hasty Tasty, located across University Avenue. It served brats, burgers, and beer, the latter in large quantities. The place had great atmosphere. Its floor was obscured by several inches of sawdust and wood shavings to soak up any beer that student drinkers spilled on the floor.

The four of us slid into a booth, ordered a pitcher of beer to get started, and began reminiscing about the summer. Time passed, and more pitchers of beer arrived and disappeared.

Not too far into the evening, conversation lagged. Helen and Bob seemed not meant for each other, and eventually, they decided to leave. Where they went, we never knew. So there we were, Sally and I, left without the purpose that had brought us there. We continued drinking and conversing about ever more weighty topics, among them her views on English literature, the quality of English Department graduate students, and of course, how things had gone that summer with the girls in her dorm. Finally, Sally said. "It's late. I think we should go." I agreed, saying I had to pay the bill.

Sally, the strong feminist she was already known to be, dug into her purse for a one-dollar bill to share the two-dollar cost of our beer. I objected, saying that she was my date, and I should pay. Despite my protests, and to prove I was the gentleman I had been raised to be, I finally graciously accepted her dollar bill. But in a sudden flash of inspiration, I proceeded to tear the bill in half and then tear the two halves in half. With that, I let the pieces flutter to the floor. There they disappeared into the thick layer of sawdust and wood shavings. Friends kidded me later that Sally must have thought I was rich!

Sally was taken aback by this dramatic act. As she started digging another dollar bill out of her purse, she insisted, "I want to pay my share of the bill because I invited you to this evening." I put a quick stop to that, saying, "I am obligated to pay because you are my date, no matter how you organized the evening." Then we both laughed and sat down to continue our conversation. Based on what we knew about each other from earlier conversations, we soon realized we had much in common. Thus, the ice was broken. We had "discovered" each other. Soon our bodies came together in a tight embrace, and our lips met in a long kiss. What a surprise to both of us that this was happening.

A Romance Begins

While walking back to the dorms and by now somewhat tipsy, I said, "Let's go down to the pier (jutting into Lake Mendota) so we can continue our conversation." Sally agreed. So there we sat, talking about ever more serious matters. We did some more smooching. The sparks flew. We concluded we were seriously interested in each other. What a strange turn of events.

The next morning our social group, including Helen and Bob, gathered in the Van Hise Dining Room for breakfast and then adjourned to the Pine Room for more coffee and goodbyes. Before departing, Sally asked that we keep in contact that fall by letters, she from Detroit where she would be teaching high-school English, and I from Madison where I would continue work on my master's degree in economics.

The following morning, Sally boarded a train for Chicago and then another that took her to Fennville, Michigan. Another favorite aunt, Ruth Barnes, picked her up and drove to her old family farmhouse on the eastern shore of Lake Michigan, just south of Saugatuck, Michigan. Sally relaxed there for a week before going on to her family home in Detroit to prepare for her fall semester of teaching.

The Plot Thickens

A few days later I received a postcard from Saugatuck with a brief message and a surprising ending: "With love, Sally." Such power in one word. *Love!* I was delighted. That evening, after spending the day putting a new roof on my parents' home, I began composing a reply. After reading my letter, I decided to rewrite it, knowing that Sally, an English teacher, would scrutinize my letter closely. Now that I had a strong romantic interest in Sally, I didn't want my first letter to make a bad impression on her.

Apparently, I passed muster because we became regular correspondents through the 1954–55 school year. Our early correspondences reflected a mixture of incredulity that we had met and surprise that we seemed to be so perfectly matched. We both lamented that writing letters was such a poor substitute for talking together. Sally admitted that she felt "hesitant about talking to you about the things you wrote in your letter. Words, especially in a letter, are so inadequate, so difficult to manage to express what you really think and feel. The thought of trying to put my feelings and thoughts into words in a letter overwhelms me. It is almost an impossible job, but I will try." She did try, and she succeeded.

I admitted that in my letter, "I was venturing into new territory, asking you to excuse any poorly stated remarks due to my inexperience." I expressed the hope I would improve with time. I went on to say, "Pleasantly, the real Sally Porch proved to be much what I had imagined and hoped her to be."

The Budding Romance

And so our romance took off as we struggled to communicate with each other via the U.S. mail. Gradually, we relaxed a bit as we became better acquainted. We corresponded regularly in the ten months that followed. We often commented on the considerable effort required to find time to write. (Let me note that Sally saved all of my letters, and I saved all of hers. A few years ago, I sorted them out, made Xerox copies, and had them bound in separate books for our daughters and whatever value they might have.)

Though physically separated, we met several times during the coming academic year—at the November Homecoming weekend in Madison, in Detroit where I attended the American Economic Association's annual meetings held immediately after Christmas, and in Detroit again during spring break. By then, I had been admitted to the Johns Hopkins University graduate program in economics. I now felt more settled about my future of becoming an academic economist.

We decided we had a bright future ahead of us. Sally gave up on her planned trip to Europe and decided to come back to Madison for the summer to take another English course. I made a similar decision, knowing I would have my master's degree completed in June.

That following summer of 1955, we both continued as dormitory house fellows, each of us charged with supervising fifty undergraduate resident students, some enrolled for serious study but many others for summer fun. We each took a course or two to keep our minds active. Most important, we had a wonderful summer together in the midst of old friends who had also returned to Madison. We received a lot of kidding about our romance. I remember one good friend regularly described me as "carrying the torch for Sally Porch." That August when summer school ended, we gathered together with friends at the Hasty Tasty to celebrate the anniversary of our memorable first date.

By then, I knew much more about Sally. She had grown up in Detroit.

Her father, James Porch, formerly an army First Lieutenant, commanded an infantry company during some of the fiercest fighting of World War I. After the war, he became a small-town banker and ended up working as an executive for Ford Motor Company. Her mother worked for several years, attending and graduating from the University of Wisconsin where she won several sports letters for her athletic prowess. She then taught physical education at Rockford College before marrying. She later taught high school physical education in Detroit and still later became a social worker. Sally's mother and two of her aunts all graduated from college—unusual at the time—and embarked on full-time careers. In doing so, they all served as role models for Sally.

Sally was known among her sorority sisters for her passionate advocacy of education and careers for women.

Sally went on to study history and graduate with honors from Wayne State University in Detroit. After beginning her teaching career with a rocky year working as a permanent substitute in Detroit's downtown schools, she decided to pursue a master's degree in English at the University of Wisconsin-Madison. Upon completing that degree, she became a full-time high school English teacher in Detroit and then Dearborn, Michigan.

Marriage Looms

In September 1955, I visited Sally in Detroit while en route to Baltimore, Maryland, where I would begin my doctoral work at Johns Hopkins. Sally visited me at Thanksgiving. We had decided earlier in November that we could not wait until the next June to be married. Instead, we would have a quiet wedding in Detroit immediately after Christmas. While in Baltimore, we bought wedding rings. And the die was cast. That marked the beginning of a long and happy marriage, two lovely daughters, fulfilling careers, and engaged lives.

In thinking back about what brought us together, I wonder whether the outcome would have differed if I could have known that Sally would suffer from dementia in her later years. I suppose that in the new world of DNA testing and early identification of dementia markers, the possibility of marrying someone destined to suffer from dementia could very well dampen their attractiveness as a possible mate. However, back then it probably would have made no difference because dementia was viewed as an old person's disease, and those years were too far off to affect my decision.

What if Sally had already become a proponent of the right to die? Might that have affected our relationship? I doubt it. I probably would have viewed her advocacy as another aspect of her feminist inclinations.

Our Nomadic Life Begins

After our marriage, Sally taught for a year and a half at Eastern High School, one of two all-girl schools in Baltimore, while I continued my graduate work. We enjoyed life in Baltimore. In August in 1957, we moved to Washington, D.C., where I had a fellowship at the Brookings Institution. By this time Sally was pregnant and did not attempt to find a teaching job. At that point, she decided to devote the coming years to raising our children and to return to teaching after our girls were well established in school.

Sally would become a devoted mother, helping to raise two intelligent and compassionate daughters, Ellen and Martha. As the youngest in her family and having had no babysitting experience, Sally's years as a young mother were not easy. Mothering did not come naturally to her. Fortunately, a warmhearted neighbor and mother of four named Freda Trunk became Sally's mentor during our early years in Los Angeles when I taught at UCLA. Years later, Sally always spoke warmly of Freda, expressing gratitude for her help and support during that crucial time. Once our daughters passed early childhood, mothering came more easily to Sally. She always arranged her teaching schedule so that she could be home when the girls arrived from school so she could talk with them about what they had learned that day and deal with the usual problems of preteens and teens. We both took a keen interest in our daughters' education, making sure one of us always went to "go-to-school" nights and attended other school activities. We regularly read to them and encouraged their love of reading. Sally loved to engage our girls in discussions and encouraged their academic interests. It is no accident that they became avid readers and later National Merit scholars.

As my professional career developed, we moved frequently. From Baltimore we went to Washington, D.C. for a year where our first daughter,

Ellen Jean, was born. From there we went to Los Angeles for three years where our second daughter, Martha Lee, was born while I taught at UCLA. We then moved from Los Angeles to Chicago for the year I spent at the University of Chicago then back to Los Angeles and UCLA for a year and a half before returning to Washington where I spent a year as a Senior Staff Economist for the President's Council of Economic Advisers (CEA). All of this moving occurred in the space of just nine years as I climbed the academic ladder. In addition to caring for the girls, Sally took every opportunity to continue learning by enrolling in courses at both UCLA and the University of Chicago.

While any young mother of two small children would have found our frequent long-distance moves stressful, the strain weighed particularly heavily on Sally. Despite her unhappiness at the prospect of each successive move, she proceeded to readily form close friendships in each place we lived. Paradoxically, while these relationships eased some of the strain of adjusting to new places, they at the same time made it that much harder to move on to the next location. Indeed, Sally would probably have been happy to have stayed in any of the places we lived—Los Angeles, Chicago, or Washington, D.C.

For some reason, Sally suffered from periodic bouts of depression that I always found worrisome. Her depression usually required a week or so of bed rest and a reduced schedule of activities in the following weeks. I always tried to be as supportive as I could. Usually, we found a psychiatrist who treated her with medication and soon had her back at full speed again.

Washington, D.C.

Returning to Washington, D.C. in 1964 offered many wonderful cultural opportunities for us as a family. For me, however, it was a grueling year. As a staff economist on the President's Council of Economic Advisers, I worked long hours and rarely arrived home early enough to join Sally and the girls for supper. From Thanksgiving until the day we departed Washington on Sally's birthday, January 23, 1965, I had only one day off—Christmas Day. The reason being was the CEA, myself included, was writing the annual *Economic Report of the President,* and we had a very tight deadline.

Sally's Views on Death and Dying

As mentioned earlier, both of Sally's parents died when she was still a young woman as did my father in the early 1970s. Again, her parents did not have easy deaths, which led us to think more about how to deal with death and end-of-life issues. Through the rest of the 1970s, Sally continued to be bothered by the lack of more compassionate ways of dealing with end-of-life issues. She was heartened when in the early 1980s, she learned about Derek Humphry's establishment of the Hemlock Society. She quickly joined, hoping its establishment would accelerate efforts by the states to enact death with dignity legislation. As Humphry's subsequent books on death and dying were published, Sally eagerly read them. They included *The Right to Die: An Historical and Legal Perspective on Euthanasia* with Ann Wickett (1987), and *Final Exit: The Practicalities of Self-Deliverance and Assisted Suicide for the Dying* (1991).

The First Unitarian Society

Sally's contribution to the Death with Dignity Movement took shape in early 1983 when she was appointed to a committee on death and dying that was to report its findings back to the First Unitarian congregation in Madison, Wisconsin. She organized an all-day workshop on death, dying, and funeral arrangements. Attendees included medical professionals and a medical ethicist as well as social workers and consumer finance experts. They all came together, along with many Unitarians, to discuss what might be done to promote more compassionate and less expensive ways of dying. They received a booklet, Final Choices: A Handbook on Funeral Arrangements (November 1983), on death and dying that Sally had taken the lead in writing. Though her fellow committee members were not ready to introduce her ideas on the right to die, they did agree to make the case for Living Wills and Declarations to Physicians.

I do remember that afterward Sally regularly grumbled when she heard about local people dying in great pain. She surmised that in most cases, they would probably have been better off if, with the help of medical assistance, they could have passed away much sooner. In other words, they could have avoided the pain, suffering, and indignity associated with dementia. Indeed,

Sally's story offers a dramatic illustration of how life plays out in the absence of right-to-die legislation.

By the late 1980s, Living Wills, and later Advanced Medical Directives gave individuals and their Durable Power of Attorney for Health Care the right to refuse certain "heroic measures" if and when they were declared terminal. After I found the American Medical Association's Living Will forms in the *Journal of the American Medical Association* in 1988, we completed them and had our lawyer include them in our Estate Plan. Sally believed doing so would provide some protection against being kept alive by artificial means such as feeding and breathing tubes. The availability of these forms stimulated more thinking and discussion about death and dying among the elderly and their families.

Not until 1997 did voters in Oregon approve a much-discussed death-with-dignity law that would under certain circumstances permit medically assisted suicides. To prevent abuses, people seeking to end their lives had to be terminal, and they had to be of sound mind—two conditions that people with moderate dementia could not meet. Subsequently, a number of other states passed similar legislation. Among them were Washington, Montana, Idaho, Vermont, and more recently California, Colorado, Hawaii, Maine, New Jersey, and the District of Columbia. Unfortunately, this legislation, as with the Oregon legislation, makes no provision for people who might suffer from dementia. They had two strikes against them: They were not immediately terminal, and they were no longer of sound mind—two requirements for individuals seeking death-with-dignity assistance.

Starting in the late 1990s, Sally and I began attending periodic meetings of the local chapter of the organization Compassion and Choices, formally the Hemlock Society, but both of us were too busy to do much more than that. These meetings sought to educate people and advocate for death-with-dignity legislation, and unfortunately, not many people attended them. Though Sally believed strongly in the right to die, she, like myself, was unable to help promote the idea of death with dignity and the legislation needed to enact it. Although she realized the importance of her right-to-die proposal, she lacked the energy required to help promote it, telling me, "Younger people will have to take up the challenge."

She would continue in her later years to do what she loved to do, namely teach. As for me, I received an unexpected tenured faculty appointment at the University of Wisconsin-Madison; the year was 1964. The Economics Department was interested in my policy experience in Washington as well as my policy-related research. Sally was most pleased, not only because she knew Madison as a wonderful place to live, more importantly, it offered, finally, the possibility of being settled rather than always being on the move.

Sally had handled my strange life in Washington quite gracefully. But before leaving D.C., she took revenge of sorts by writing a poem to the tune of "Without You" from the then-hit My Fair Lady. In a memorandum addressed to my CEA colleagues, I wrote: "Though my wife, Sally, and I enjoyed our stay in Washington, she has had many, many hours of solitude in which to reflect on the economy, the CEA, and related matters." The poem spoofed me and my work for the CEA, and when it was sung by the wives of the male CEA employees to their husbands, it was quite the hit!

On to Madison

Sally and I were sad to leave our old friends behind but excited to begin a new life in Wisconsin. We arrived there on a cold, snowy day in late January 1965. We soon bought a house situated close to Shorewood Hills Elementary School, which our two girls attended. As I resumed my academic life, Sally's long-suppressed energy was suddenly unleashed. She quickly joined and participated actively in the newly formed women's advocacy group, National Organization for Women (NOW), became deeply involved in League of Women Voters issues and joined a women's book club that still meets today. In addition, she trained as a junior Great Books discussion leader. Soon we joined in organizing an always-stimulating adult Great Books discussion group that continued meeting for the next forty years.

Given Sally's love of learning and language, she regularly quoted memorable lines from such literary giants as Dickens, Shakespeare, and Wordsworth. She also read widely and was heavily influenced by feminist writers, among them Virginia Woolf, the French writers Collete and Simone de Beauvoir, as well as American feminist writers, beginning with Betty Friedan in the mid-1960s.

She had always been a skillful conversationalist, offering bold though well-supported opinions and having little tolerance for pomposity or sentimentality. Being that she had grown up as a strong advocate for women, Sally was never afraid to express her feminist views to either friend or foe. Her sense of humor was delightful, and she had a keen appreciation for the ironies of life. Her deep interest in other people was apparent in her multiple networks of friends. They typically described her as warm, funny, strong-willed, smart, highly verbal, well-educated, and intellectually curious. I like to think that we shared many of these same qualities, which helped sustain our long and happy marriage.

Sally often accompanied me on travels related to my appointments at universities in other countries as well as national and international conferences. Through the years, we also traveled extensively internationally to visit family and friends in—among other places—England, Scotland, Norway, Sweden, South Arica, Germany, Poland, Italy, and Mexico. We took part in a number of elderhostels, both here and abroad, specifically in Alaska, Russia, Italy, Ireland, and Eastern Europe.

Whether as a stimulating wife and companion, an excellent English teacher and mentor to students, or a creative and intellectually challenging mother and grandmother, Sally's lifelong ability to engage others with her conversational skills proved to be an important factor in her professional success. It also contributed to *our* professional success, our success as a couple, and the success we had in raising two accomplished daughters and later developing close relationships with our four grandchildren.

Sally and I really were, in so many ways, a perfect match. In December 2015, we celebrated our sixtieth wedding anniversary, only a couple of months before she passed away on March 10, 2016.

Chapter 3

LAST DAYS AT HOME

Early Signs

Initially, I didn't attach great importance to Sally's occasional memory lapses, such as forgetting people's names or her difficulty recalling past events. I assumed they represented the normal forgetfulness associated with aging. Likewise, the repetition that began to mark her conversations, not uncommon for people her age, did not set off any alarms.

However, in early 2006, she began forgetting such things as medical appointments, meeting friends for coffee, remembering how to get to familiar destinations around Madison, and at times, even forgetting where she'd planned to go. At an international elderhostel in Ireland in spring 2007, she confessed to me that she could no longer keep track of the names of our fellow travelers, something she'd always prided herself on doing. On another international elderhostel a year later, she had even more difficulty; she could no longer engage in conversations with other travelers. With both family members and friends, she became noticeably more repetitive in her conversations.

"I never want to hear you say that word again!" Sally shouted at me. We were sitting in her doctor's office. Various charts on the wall, the doctor's desk, and a blood pressure machine welcomed us to this familiar place. On this occasion, we were not, however, greeted by Sally's beloved doctor who had retired. We were instead in the process of becoming acquainted with his recommended colleague. When he asked her to summarize her health problems, Sally neglected to mention her memory loss, so I chimed in with, "I think she is beginning to suffer from dementia."

When friends had experienced similar memory problems in the past, Sally and I noticed. We had different friends, and after a social event, we would share our encounters over dinner or an occasional glass of wine at home. "He seemed to be having memory problems, probably dementia," Sally once said of a good friend. We had always had long discussions about dementia and the right to die. As always, she was a steadfast advocate that those with dementia should have the right to die as their dementia gradually worsened. Of course, this is a choice that needed to be made prior to the onset of dementia or in its earliest stages.

After Sally's insistence of not to mention the word *dementia* again, the doctor looked at me quizzically and then continued his discussion with her. I had no idea Sally would take such offense at the word, but then again she was well known for her blunt and direct way of expressing herself. Of course, who would want to hear that they have dementia? It would be much like someone with a chronic mental illness being told they have schizophrenia. There is a deep-rooted resistance of accepting such a diagnosis.

There and then I decided to respect her wish. I suspected that despite her loss of memory she would not forget my bringing up the subject of her dementia until her memory was completely gone. So I began referring to her problem as *memory loss*—a term she found quite acceptable. Not until sometime in 2011, after famed women's basketball coach Pat Summitt's public announcement of her diagnosis of dementia, did Sally finally feel comfortable using the word *dementia* even though three years had passed since her official diagnosis.

As time went on, I was less dismissive of Sally's memory loss. She'd always had a good memory. So did I. In fact, friends often remarked, and still do, at the sharpness of my mind and my ability to recall obscure information and long-ago events. I consider myself lucky.

Sally's Depression

A year after meeting with her new primary care physician, Sally had a change in psychiatrists. As mentioned before, in early 2008, we met with her new psychiatrist. He replaced her recently retired former psychiatrist who had dealt with Sally's periodic episodes of depression for several decades. This is another sign of aging: One experiences not only the loss of friends and relatives but the loss of healthcare providers. Losing two doctors in a single year meant that their intimate knowledge of Sally's health and health problems was lost as well. Finding replacements proved difficult because Sally was fussy about what kind of person she wanted to oversee her health. In fact, she tried several doctors and several psychiatrists before she found new ones to her liking.

What triggered her depression could never be explained. We never knew its root cause, but that is not uncommon. Depression is a complex disease that can be caused by and related to a multitude of internal and external issues. Her first bout with depression had occurred in January 1959, about ten months after the birth of our first daughter, Ellen. We had only recently arrived in Los Angeles. I was busy at my teaching job at UCLA and launching my research. We knew almost nobody. Sally found it difficult to be home alone and responsible for a young child, probably because she had no experience with young children. She was very nervous and anxious about Ellen's upbringing and was constantly worried whether or not she was doing the right thing. Soon a colleague recommended a psychiatrist who helped Sally recover her balance. From time to time, however, throughout the rest of our married lives, Sally became depressed and was greatly helped by antidepressants and by a psychiatrist in Madison whom she began seeing in 1967 and continued seeing from time to time until his retirement in 2006.

When Sally experienced her first bout of depression, I was terrified. Not only was she listless but she seemed unable to adequately care for our now ten-month-old daughter. Fortunately, I was able to spend considerable time at home because of the late January break in the schedule of regular classes. I learned much through that experience, and with each future bout of Sally's depression I was better prepared to give my wife the help she needed. In looking back, I think she was most prone to depression when a sudden change occurred in her life. Changes of this nature included her giving birth to Ellen, our move to a new city, or the onset of a major health problem. Whenever one of these events occurred, I did my best to ease her family and household responsibilities.

After this new psychiatrist learned about Sally's now more-apparent memory problems, he recommended a memory test. In subsequent months, Sally kept wondering who had scheduled this test and why it had been scheduled. She frequently glanced at our calendar of upcoming appointments on the desk in our dining room and asked specifically about that particular appointment. I worried that she might want to back out of the test. However, in September, when the day finally arrived, Sally fully engaged in it and its various facets, which culminated with an MRI brain scan.

Official Diagnosis

In October 2008, we learned the results of Sally's memory test, which was conducted by the doctor who served as director of the Wisconsin Alzheimer's Disease Research Institute at the UW-Madison Hospital. The first part of the test revealed "mild cognitive memory loss," which was not surprising to me. The second part, involving the MRI, proved to be more ominous. It revealed considerable buildup of amyloid plaque in her brain, indicating "subcortical vascular dementia."

With all the mystery about dementia and the many unknowns that may cause it, combined with uncertainty about who will be affected by it, the need for legalizing a person's right to die is quite apparent. Such legislation would allow an individual, fearful of eventually suffering from dementia, to specify when in their journey through dementia they would want to have their life medically and painlessly terminated. We need to develop a more routine and acceptable right to die. Doing so will help insulate people from the unknown future.

The subcortical vascular dementia that Sally was diagnosed with is one of the numerous forms of dementia that include Alzheimer's disease, the most common type. Dementia is a broad term, often called an umbrella term, which refers to deterioration in brain function. The symptoms can include declines in thought processes, judgment, reasoning, memory, communication, and aberrant behavior.

Dementia initially affects short-term memory, followed by difficulty in finding the right words, poor judgment, or strange changes in behaviors and emotions. Executive functioning, such as planning or carrying out multiple steps to complete a task, may become difficult, and orientation to the day, date, time, or location may decline. Dementia is typically progressive, meaning these functions decline over time. However, such declines vary significantly based on which conditions are causing the dementia. The risk of developing dementia increases as people age but it is not a normal outcome of aging. More than half of the population over the age of eighty-five develop Alzheimer's disease. Indeed, more than 5.7 million Americans suffer from Alzheimer's or another kind of dementia.

The doctor explained that no cure for dementia existed. The best that could be said is that two medications, Aricept and Namenda, had shown some success in slowing its advance. Taking these medications seemed like a good move, and they were prescribed for Sally.

Sally took the news of her diagnosis quite calmly, at least outwardly. It was as if she already knew and understood the diagnosis and that nothing could be done but to accept the fact. Her major concern was Alzheimer's disease. The doctor assured her that he found no evidence of that disease, and given her age, the odds were strongly against her becoming afflicted with it.

The doctor's diagnosis of dementia did not surprise me. Indeed, it served as a rationale for Sally's wide-ranging symptoms, which I had observed over the past two-plus years. Nevertheless, I wondered what this would mean for me and how my responsibilities for Sally's care would evolve. The uncertainties were most unsettling, as I imagined I might never know what state she might be in when I visited her in a care facility, nor would I know how long it would be before her final decline began.

Rather than curse my fate, I realized I needed to begin learning as much as I could about dementia and how to best care for Sally in the coming years. I realized that my caregiving responsibilities would continue as long as Sally remained alive. Thus, I began reading everything I could find on the subject.

I tried to learn as much as I could by attending local lectures and workshops, including the highly informative workshops taught by Teepa Snow, an expert on coping with the often-strange behaviors of people experiencing dementia. Snow makes frequent appearances and offers excellent advice at workshops around the country, including several I attended in Madison.

Why Sally?

What the diagnosis did was prompt me to ask, why Sally? What had caused her dementia? I puzzled over these questions from time to time as I sat in my reading chair in our living room. The best time to ponder these questions was late in the evening after Sally was already in bed and asleep. Why had she developed dementia, but I had not? How would I manage her care? What would I do after she passed away? How would our daughters handle the demise and death of their mother? All these questions swirled through my mind. I didn't see how religion would help, nor was I sure that our membership in the First Unitarian Society would provide any answers. Instead, it seemed to me that I would have to take a pragmatic approach and attempt to learn as much as I could from others who had similar experiences and had to confront these same questions.

Sally's relatives and friends expressed surprise when they observed her decline and learned of her diagnosis. Based on the then-prevailing wisdom about what elderly people should do to ward it off, Sally had performed well on all counts. She lived an active and engaged intellectual life. After retiring from her teaching career, she had continued to teach English as a second language. She enjoyed participating in a wide range of physical activities. She maintained regular contact with several networks of friends drawn from her professional and social circles. She continued to be conscious of what it took to maintain her health, eating well-balanced meals in moderation.

As a lifelong teacher, one who continually sought new ways to engage her students and help them learn, Sally's mental life was vigorous and dynamic. Well into retirement, Sally continued to stay mentally active in other important ways. She kept abreast of the news, regularly consuming the contents of the local and national newspapers we subscribed to.

She continued to read for her two book groups and to participate with me in our ever-stimulating Great Books discussion group that met monthly. She gathered regularly with several groups of friends for animated, wide-ranging discussions. We continued attending campus lectures, going to plays and concerts, and attending church services. And, as mentioned earlier in chapter 1, the two of us loved to play Scrabble together.

Sally's busy life of the mind did not come at the expense of her body. Throughout her teaching career, Sally exercised regularly. Five days a week over the course of many years, she met with various friends and neighbors to take vigorous morning walks. When back problems worsened as she approached retirement, she switched to an 8:00 a.m., forty-minute, warm-water pool exercise class three times a week. Her social life continued unabated. Following her morning pool sessions, she invariably stopped at the nearby Starbucks coffee shop for her usual latte and conversations with other regular customers as well as the friendly young baristas.

Sally was quick to share with others the dietary precepts instilled by her mother, namely three meals a day, nothing to eat after dinner, no snacks between meals, and no sugar. The latter instruction was ironic because she had a pronounced weakness for chocolate in whatever form it was available. She enjoyed having a glass of wine with our evening dinners. Until the last several years of her life, Sally's weight varied no more than a pound or two over what she'd weighed when we were married.

Sally nevertheless experienced a variety of continuing health problems, many of them long-standing but usually manageable with the help of medication. But that was not true for her lower back problems, her restless legs syndrome, her nutcracker esophagus problem, and her high cholesterol. In her seventies, she had two knee replacements and cataract surgeries on both eyes. Yet none of these health problems seemed in any way related to the emergence of her dementia.

Why dementia struck Sally remains a mystery to this day.

Early Caregiving

The diagnosis of dementia forced me to rethink my role as Sally's caregiver. I realized I already was a caregiver and had been playing that role for almost two years. In fact, I had considerable experience, having cared for her during her periodic bouts of depression. After Sally's dementia diagnosis, I began paying much closer attention to her health and welfare. I began monitoring her medications, kept track of her medical appointments, always accompanied her on these appointments, took detailed notes at these meetings, and made virtually all of her healthcare decisions. My main responsibilities were to urge her to follow her doctor's instructions, pick up her new prescriptions, and make certain she took her medications as instructed. I also realized that because of her memory lapses, I needed to be a strong and effective advocate for my wife.

I knew that her condition would worsen over time and that I would have to reconcile myself to that reality. I soon abandoned my office space in the Economics Department and continued my writing and research in a spacious office at home. I did this so that I could hear and monitor Sally's movements on the floor above my study. To my surprise, I did not miss my involvement with my colleagues in the Economics Department. By this time I had been retired for more than a decade, and the department was staffed with many new people working on problems that were not all that interesting to me. In addition, I kept busy pursing my own research projects and interests.

During this time, I made a point to keep Sally informed of my whereabouts and to limit my time away from home. I also needed to keep better records of Sally's condition and any significant events related to her dementia. This posed no difficulties because I regularly wrote detailed accounts of her meetings with her physician and other medical personnel.

Because of Sally's back problems, more than a decade earlier, we had added a downstairs bedroom and bath. As an added precaution, I had our house inspected and modifications made that would keep us safe. These modifications included more safety bars in the bathrooms, handrails on both sides of the stairs leading to the basement and to the second floor, the removal of rugs on which both she and I might slip and fall, better lighting both inside and outside the house, and an iron railing on our home's front steps.

By mid-2010, I had become Sally's full-time caregiver. A caregiver has no road map to follow when thrust into this new territory where surprises and disappointments abound. For better or worse, like marriage, caregiving became a process of "learning by doing." But, as the experts say, every case is different—that's the way this disease plays out. A caregiver hardly needs to be reminded of this reality. All a caregiver can do is try to keep on top of things. This means "learning on the fly" as much as possible, hoping to become a better caregiver, focusing on what seems to work, and avoiding efforts that don't. Being in contact with other caregivers can be most useful in figuring out what works best.

As Sally's cognitive abilities faded, my full-time caregiving duties were not as great a challenge for me as they may have been for other husbands in similar situations. I could easily handle the household chores. While growing up, my brothers and I had learned an array of homemaking skills, including cooking, washing clothes, ironing shirts, sewing on buttons, house cleaning, and making home repairs. During our married life, I always tried to do as much as I could to help around the house. Not long after Sally had retired in the early 1990s, I had gradually taken over more of the cooking and house maintenance activities because she no longer enjoyed doing them. Many of them she could no longer do, being impeded by her back problems and her weakening knees.

During the early years of her dementia, I was able to leave the house to have lunch with friends and colleagues, participate in book discussions, attend campus lectures, and depart for a morning or afternoon to do research on campus. My being away did not bother Sally. She rarely complained about my absences, and I always tried to keep them relatively short to keep better track of how she was doing.

By 2010, I began to notice other changes. Sally's interest in her women's book group declined. Her interest in our Great Books discussion group faded. Her meetings with friends tapered off, and she no longer wanted to go to her warm-water pool exercise classes. In short, the expanding symptoms of Sally's dementia finally forced her to make significant changes in her daily life.

Though our married life was a happy one, it had always thrived because we allowed each other to pursue separate professional interests and yet maintain a strong interest in what the other was doing. In addition, we always ate our meals together unless we had other arrangements with friends or colleagues. Much of our evening conversations at dinner involved comparing notes about our work and social activities. So although we followed our own callings, we remained closely connected by our interests in each other's work and related activities. These connections weakened as Sally's memory failed, but they did not lessen our love and attraction for one another.

Troubling Challenges

Several serious problems emerged as Sally's dementia worsened. One was her increasingly erratic driving. A second was an increase in her alcohol consumption. A third was a reoccurrence of her periodic episodes of depression. Trying to understand how and even whether these problems were linked proved to be difficult. Figuring out what could or should be done about them proved to be even more difficult.

As Sally's memory problems became more apparent, her driving skills began to deteriorate. Beginning in 2007, she began receiving citations for minor traffic violations, such as not wearing her seat belt, speeding, or not coming to a full stop at intersections. In succeeding years, she experienced several fender benders, once running into a large landscaping boulder along the edge of a street not far from our home; this collision caused substantial damage to our car. By this time, I began worrying that she might cause or be in a serious accident. I discussed my concerns about her driving with her and her need for greater caution. Our two daughters who visited us in the spring of 2009 also voiced concern about her driving, and they, too, spoke to her about it.

Sally acknowledged these concerns, but they had no effect on her driving. I was reluctant to force her to give up her driver's license. As a Detroiter whose father had worked for the Ford Motor Company, she was wedded to the automobile.

In early 2010, Sally received several additional traffic citations, two of them involving minor collisions with other cars. After the first citation, our auto insurance company sent a letter to us expressing its concern about her driving. After the third citation, the Shorewood Hills police reported her to the Department of Motor Vehicles, which in early 2010 had already threatened to cancel her driver's license.

In response to these developments, I contacted Sally's primary care doctor, asking him to talk to Sally about her driving. To my great relief, he managed to convince her to give up her license, citing the dangers of causing a serious accident. The timing was fortunate because only a few days later, the Department of Motor Vehicles informed us that it had revoked her license. Sally was most unhappy that she was no longer able to drive.

The second and in many ways more serious challenge involved dealing with Sally's increased consumption of alcohol. Over the course of our marriage, we did drink, but not a great deal, mostly a glass of wine with dinner and quite limited social drinking outside the house. Some years after her retirement, Sally and a group of her longtime women friends started gathering weekly for pre-dinner cocktails. This went on for several years, but at some point, probably in 2007 or 2008, Sally's usual one drink turned into two drinks. About that time, I noticed that when she arrived home after these get-togethers, she was not only less articulate but also less steady on her feet. I reminded her that most of her medications warned against consuming alcohol, as did her doctors, because of potential adverse drug interactions. Sally promised to restrain herself, but that did not happen.

Sally's alcohol consumption was a confounding factor that helped to obscure what was actually happening to her during the gradual onset of her dementia. Drinking can lead to depression, and depression can lead to drinking. Both can contribute to memory loss. In 2009, on a visit to our daughter Martha in Albuquerque, Sally had stashed several miniature bottles of alcohol in her luggage, which somehow escaped the notice of the TSA. Perceiving this behavior to be an alarming symptom of addiction, Martha and I sat down with Sally to have a serious talk about her drinking. Among other things, we discussed the fact that her alcohol consumption seemed to be adversely affecting her memory.

Sally heard us out but did not change her behavior. Indeed, alcohol seemed the logical and obvious explanation for both her memory loss and the impairment of her driving ability. Thus, Sally's alcohol consumption became my primary concern. At that point, I took steps to ensure that Sally's access to it was cut off.

The revocation of Sally's driver's license was a major psychological blow to her. The freedom she had enjoyed throughout her entire adult life—to drive wherever and whenever she wanted—had ended. No more mid-afternoon drives to Starbucks for a latte. No more sudden decisions to head out for a movie. No more quick trips to buy something needed to round out the evening's dinner menu. Though I expressed my willingness to transport her wherever she might want to go, it was a poor substitute for the freedom she had previously experienced. Losing her driver's license, triggered, I believe, a recurrence of the episodic depression Sally had experienced throughout her adult life.

Sally's Depression Deepens

To reduce Sally's drinking, I removed the liquor from our liquor cabinet. I soon discovered she was buying miniature bottles of vodka while driving home from her morning exercise sessions, hiding them in various places around the house and then masking her drinking at home by her need for "ice water." Finally—and thankfully—after she lost her driver's license she could no longer make these liquor purchases and thus could not continue her surreptitious drinking. Her wish to maintain her access to alcohol may have been another reason for her reluctance to discontinue driving. Perhaps she experienced an awareness of the fact that her life was changing and that she was changing. She also had some depression and anxiety, and alcohol likely helped calm her fears and pass the time.

In November 2010, she became extremely depressed, so much so that she talked about taking her own life. My daughters became concerned and contacted her doctor, who had her sent to the UW Hospital Psychiatric Ward for observation. Being in the psychiatric ward did not work, however. The medication she was put on did more harm than good, increasing her agitation and starting an allergic reaction that greatly upset her. With the help of her doctor, we got her released from the psychiatric ward. It took some time before the effects of that medication wore off.

Sally's verbal and social skills proved to be another confounding factor. Because Sally remained quite capable of engaging in active (albeit increasingly repetitive) conversation, dementia did not suggest itself as the culprit in her memory loss. It also seemed possible that her memory loss and conversational repetition were simply the byproducts of normal aging that were being exacerbated by her drinking and/or her depression. We thought that if either or both of those problems could be controlled, her cognitive abilities might improve. Her depression, therefore, became the primary focus of her doctor.

My guess is that her dementia contributed to both her careless driving as well as her desire to drink. In retrospect, I acknowledge that I could have been—and should have been—more aggressive in dealing with the situation. I'm sure that earlier on I could have convinced her doctor to recommend to the DMV that her license be revoked. Yet, as a longtime husband, taking such direct action seemed to violate our mutual trust. She most certainly would have been outraged. At the time, the risk of an accident seemed less frightening than facing Sally's anger and the inevitable lashing out at me from her anger.

This period—2007 to 2010—was for me the most difficult part of Sally's journey through dementia. Among the elderly, the problem of driving, one that many families struggle with, is a touchy issue in and of itself. Dementia in elderly drivers is undoubtedly a common problem as well, but little advice is offered to family caregivers on how to confront these two issues. Add drinking (and the accompanying denial) to the picture, as was the case with Sally, and the scenario becomes still more complicated and difficult to address. I must admit that I could not figure out how to best handle this whole state of affairs. The trust that Sally and I had always shared was breaking down. How could that trust be maintained when Sally, because of her dementia and depression, was no longer the person she once was?

Lee and Sally, Housefellows at UW, summer 1955

Lee and Sally, Wedding day, Detroit 1955

Ellen, Martha, and Sally, Shorewood Hills, 1967

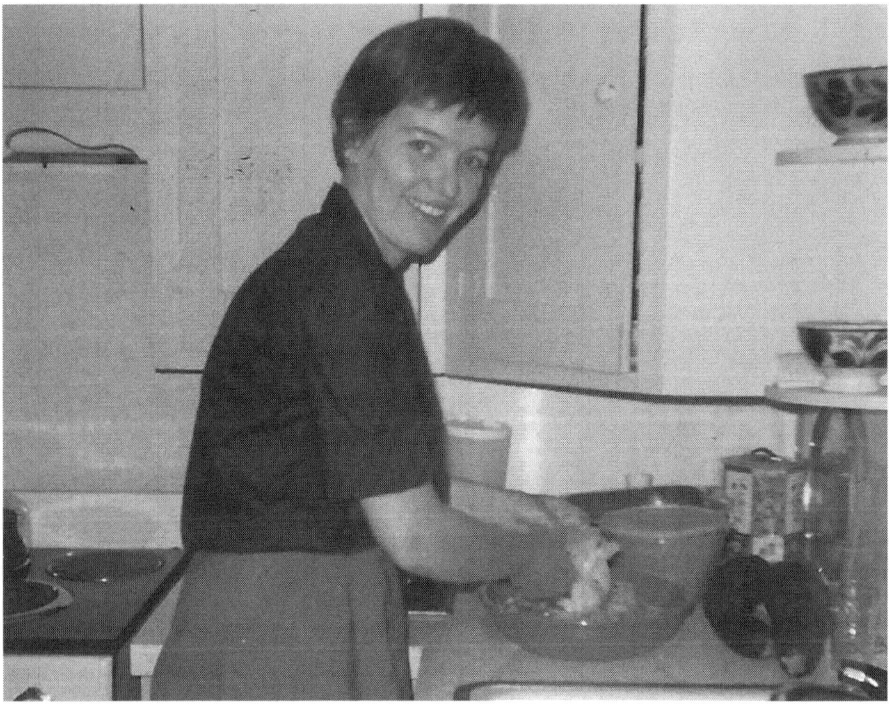

Sally in the kitchen, Summer 1968

Sally teaching at MATC, Madison, 1975

Sally and her ESL students, Madison WI 1995

Lee and Sally in the United Kingdom, 1997

Lee and Sally, Alaskan cruise, 1999

Sally at MATC, Madison, 1993

Sally and Ivan,
Shorewood Hills, 2010

50th wedding anniversary, Johannesburg, 2005

50th wedding anniversary, December 2005

Lee and Sally,
60th wedding
anniversary, Madison, 2015

Sally at Brightstar,
October 2015

Part II

Transitions

"The Lake Isle of Innisfree" by William Butler Yeats

I will arise and go now, and go to Innisfree,
And a small cabin build there, of clay and wattles made:
Nine bean-rows will I have there, a hive for the honey-bee:
And live alone in the bee-loud glade.

And I shall have some peace there,
for peace comes dropping slow,
Dropping from the walls of the morning to
where the cricket sings;
There midnight's all a glimmer, and noon a purple glow,
And evening full of the linnet's wings.

I will arise and go now, for always night and day
I hear lake water lapping with low sounds by the shore:
While I stand on the roadway, or on the pavements grey,
I hear it in the deep heart's core.

Chapter 4

MOVING TO ASSISTED LIVING

BEING SALLY'S CAREGIVER did not require my being constantly in Sally's presence. The frequency of her falls increased in 2011, and in early 2012, I decided to experiment by having someone come in and provide companion care when I was away. I selected a middle-aged woman who was a family friend and a former student of Sally's from many years earlier. She had experience helping to care for her mother who suffered from dementia for many years and also her father who required extensive medical care before he passed away.

The idea was simple: She would spend time interacting with Sally when I was away. But this plan did not work. Sally seemed to think it was her job to entertain the companion rather than the other way around, resulting in frustration for both of them. After such an inauspicious beginning, I decided this approach was not viable. There seemed to be no pressing need to pursue this approach because we were still managing reasonably well by ourselves.

A New Phase

Beginning in late 2011, Sally began to experience more frequent falls. One resulted in a deep gash just above her right eyebrow. When I returned home from church one Sunday morning, I found a trail of blood leading into our bedroom from our back living room, where she had fallen. I assumed that in getting up from her comfortable chair she fainted and fell against the baseboard. She had put a towel against her bleeding forehead and climbed into bed. I immediately got her up and over to the UW Hospital Emergency Room. Closing her wound required between eight and ten stitches. She was quickly released, and I drove her back home.

Another major fall occurred in early 2012 when she emerged from her morning shower while I was preparing breakfast in the kitchen. On hearing several loud thuds, I rushed to the bathroom. I found her sprawled on the bathroom floor, blood gushing from her left temple. I quickly realized she had broken an artery in her temple. I phoned 9-1-1, and the Shorewood Village Emergency Service quickly responded. The EMS crew rapidly checked her over, loaded her into their EMS vehicle, and drove her to the nearby UW Health Emergency Room.

When I arrived, an ER nurse was holding his thumb against Sally's temple to stem the flow of blood. It took an additional hour before it finally coagulated. Because of concern about a possible head injury, she had another CT scan. Though no injury was found, the results showed further deterioration, with her dementia described as somewhere between "moderate" and "severe." As with the first fall, she was soon released, and we left to have lunch back at home. Sally almost fell backward as we mounted the half-dozen steps from the garage to the first floor of our house. Fortunately, I was immediately behind her and able to push her forward so she could continue up the steps.

Whenever Sally fell or was about to fall, my quick intervention prevented this from happening on several occasions. My guess is that her falls were caused by her passing out as a result of small strokes, or perhaps these episodes may have been the result of minor seizures. What most impressed me was the difficulty of easing Sally's deadweight body onto the floor or trying to help get her back up into a standing position after she had fallen.

Fortunately, none of these mishaps resulted in any serious injury. Providing this type of help to my wife increased the risk of injuring myself, but fortunately, my strength and balance enabled me to deal with her falls. In one or two cases, I had to call on a neighbor for help. Sally may have escaped any injury only because she was so physically strong as a result of her years of regular exercise. With this history of falling it was no surprise that as she moved through various kinds of institutional care later on, staff members took strong measures to prevent this from happening again.

Changes to Sally's Lifestyle

In late spring of 2012, Sally had another severe bout with depression, more back pain, and great difficulty sleeping. Again, there seemed to be no obvious reason for this development except by this time, she had experienced several of the aforementioned falls and fainting spells. I also believe she was more keenly aware of the worsening of her dementia.

Understanding that Sally's condition was deteriorating, her psychiatrist immediately told us to eliminate most of her prescription drugs and all of her over-the-counter medications. She also prescribed powerful pain and sleeping medications for Sally. After only a couple of days, Sally bounced out of her depression and seemed more like her old, upbeat self.

The combination of dementia and depression probably accounted for the reduced range of activities she enjoyed. As already mentioned, in the fall of 2010, she began having difficulty meeting with her English as a Second Language conversational partner, in this case a young woman from Turkey. Sally had always enjoyed these weekly meetings but now found herself unable to prepare for them. Soon she became too embarrassed to continue this form of teaching. Her Turkish student asked me what she might do to help. I told her that nothing could be done. This ended Sally's formal teaching career. At long last, dementia had triumphed.

About this same time, Sally cut back on social visits with her many groups of friends. She no longer read books for her book club meetings, and she gradually reduced her daily newspaper reading. In short, her interests steadily narrowed, and she spent more and more time sitting in her chair or sleeping on the sofa.

Throughout our married life, Sally the film buff regularly went to the movies, often by herself. In 2009, her movie-going began dropping off. Then, following the loss of her driver's license in 2010, she could no longer head off to see movies on her own. It was now necessary for me to take her to the few movies she really wanted to see and view them with her. I recall in early 2011 taking her to see *Salmon Fishing in the Yemen*, and a short time later, *The Best Exotic Marigold Hotel*. After seeing these films, Sally admitted she could not follow their plots and experienced difficulty understanding the dialogue. By this time, she was no longer reading movie reviews to help her decide which movies to attend, and that was the end of her movie-going.

Another indicator of Sally's decline could be observed in our Scrabble playing. As mentioned earlier, both of us were lifelong players and greatly enjoyed the challenges posed by the game. We had often played together during the early years of our marriage, and when our children became old enough to play, we introduced them to Scrabble. Much later, we did the same with our grandchildren.

As Sally's dementia worsened and we cut back on our activities away from home, we resumed our Scrabble playing. I regularly kept score, dated the score sheets, and let them accumulate in the Scrabble box. When I recently happened upon them, I noticed we played once a week throughout 2011, roughly every other week in the first half of 2012, and less than half as frequently in the second half of 2012. We played only twice in 2013, both times in the first two months of the year. That was it. Sally didn't want to play anymore because she could no longer recall the words that were necessary to successfully play the game. What a sad development that was.

What was happening alerted me to seriously think about moving to a retirement community, one that offered an array of care opportunities that could accommodate the further declines in Sally's health that I expected would follow.

Our Relocation

Sally and I knew that after the onset of her dementia we would eventually need to move to a retirement community. However, when we could move depended on the availability of an independent living apartment. In late

March 2013, we received word that an independent living apartment in the Oakwood Village retirement community was available for us. Oakwood Village is a long-established retirement center, located in a lovely tree-filled campus. It contains a large building of independent living apartments, an assisted living facility, as well as a memory care and skilled nursing facility. We were pleased because it offered a continuum of care, including independent living, assisted living, memory care, and finally skilled nursing care. This combination would work well for Sally as her condition deteriorated.

With a mid-May move-in date, the timing was just right. Over the previous few months, it had become clear to me that I could no longer continue to provide the level of care and supervision Sally required. The Oakwood staff decided it needed an updated assessment of her cognitive skills and had her take the St. Louis University Mental Skills test (SLUMS). When Sally had taken this test several years earlier, she registered "mild" cognitive deficiency; this time she could not complete the test, which did not surprise me.

This result ruled out her being able to live with me in the independent-living apartment we had selected together. Instead, she would be moved into Tabor Oaks Assisted Living Care with the distinct possibility she might have to be moved soon afterward to Covenant Oaks Memory Care (both of which were part of Oakwood Village). I decided to move her to Tabor Oaks immediately so she could get settled in her new surroundings and remain undisturbed by the commotion of the moving process.

Sally moved into Tabor Assisted Living on April 1, 2013, with the help of our daughter, Ellen, and one of our granddaughters, Tessa Dunham, who drove up from Chicago. We furnished Sally's room with some of her favorite furniture and room decorations, trying to make it seem as much as possible like home. But she was not happy there. She participated in some group activities conducted on her floor and in the commons areas in Tabor's first floor Great Room. However, the distances she had to walk were formidable. Because most of the residents eating in its separate dining room were impaired, Sally had difficulty adjusting to that environment. Not surprisingly, she felt strongly that she did not belong there.

More Behavioral Issues

It soon became apparent to the Tabor staff that Sally needed more care and greater supervision. On several occasions, she became lost in the Oakwood Village complex. On another occasion or two, she wandered out of the Tabor building, and on still other occasions, the staff found her walking the hallways at night wearing nothing more than a light nightgown. Because these episodes indicated a loss of judgment and general coping abilities, the staff concluded the assisted-living environment was not adequate to serve Sally's needs.

Exactly one month later, the staff moved Sally and her belongings to Oakwood's Covenant Memory Care unit. She was placed in an attractive room that looked out into an enclosed courtyard. Sally was deeply upset by this move and angrily blamed me for allowing it to happen. She said that I had betrayed her trust and added that "our relationship would never be the same." Indeed, she suggested that I had placed her there in an effort to save money, an idea that could not have been further from the truth.

Sally's immediate anger soon passed, but she remained unhappy in memory care. Her dissatisfaction seemed attributable in part to complaints expressed by several other residents who referred to the place as "a prison." Why? Because Covenant was a locked facility, the purpose being to prevent residents from wandering about and getting lost. Residents could not enter or leave unless accompanied by a staff member or family member.

With the aid of her walker, Sally regularly roamed the corridors seeking a way out. She asked repeatedly why the doors were kept locked. This line of questioning ended only when an inspired staff member told Sally that the doors were locked to keep the unit's two resident cats from escaping, a brilliant explanation that finally satisfied her. However, she remained unhappy in her new residence. Sally's misery was made more apparent on a day I was visiting her when she again pleaded with me to help her to die. As we know, there was absolutely nothing I could do, given that no right-to-die legislation existed in Wisconsin. This was a plea that I would hear many times from my wife in the days and weeks ahead.

I tried to focus on more positive things and was relieved when the time came for me to move into the independent living apartment I had selected.

I moved in late May 2013. I was now only a five-minute walk away from Sally's room, and I stopped by to see her frequently, often eating meals with her. This gave me a good opportunity to observe her adjustment as well as her interaction with staff members and other residents. During these visits, I often discussed Sally's adjustment with both the resident assistants and the professional staff—the nurse manager, social worker, other nurses and the caregiver staff—as well as other caregivers when they visited their families.

In the first couple of months, Sally participated in only a few of the many organized activities offered there. At my prompting, the staff made a greater effort to get her involved. I tried to help by attending some activities with her. Still, Sally regularly expressed a desire to return home to the house that I had sold and was no longer ours. I brought Sally to my independent living apartment several times, but she showed little interest in it or even in her beloved cat, Ivan.

Agitation Increases

Although the staff reported a few incidents of Sally's agitated behavior in the first two months of her residence in Covenant Memory Care, neither they nor I regarded this behavior as serious. However, I had noticed some aberrant behavior at mealtime, such as trying to force the old fellow next to her to talk and wondering loudly why a woman who suffered from Parkinson's disease had to be fed by her husband. Sally was engaging in inappropriate social behavior, saying and doing things she would never have dreamed of doing in her previous life.

Since Sally always had a tendency to speak her mind, I often found it difficult to distinguish behaviors that were simply products of her personality traits, perhaps now a bit more pronounced than before, from the symptoms of dementia. In retrospect, I may have been too prone to ascribe Sally's poor behavior to the former rather than realizing it was a sign of her worsening illness.

Early in August 2013, I asked for a three-month evaluation of Sally's adaptation to Covenant's Memory Care unit. I wanted to know more about her behavior as perceived by the staff. The nurse manager, the day nurse, the social worker, and the director of assisted living met with me and our daughter, Ellen, in a conference room to review Sally's situation. The staff reported some agitation and anxiety, more on weekends than during the week. Some staff thought my Saturday morning visits or my taking Sally out for a ride or to lunch stirred her up and led to more anxiety later in the day. On Sundays, when there were fewer group activities, Sally would become even more agitated, often yelling and cursing at both staff members and other residents. While the staff expressed some concern, they voiced a hope that with more time, Sally would adapt. Thus, I felt no great alarm about Sally's behavior.

Chapter 5

AGITATION AND SEROQUEL

Agitation and Aggression Increase

In mid-September 2013, Sally began to display increased agitation and anxiety, as well as erratic behavior typical of people with worsening dementia. The staff became more and more concerned about her ever-more aggressive behavior, which included crashing into other residents with her walker and invading other people's rooms. This behavior escalated through the rest of the month and accelerated in early October. Both the staff and I noticed that Sally now spent less time walking, and when she did, her speed had slowed appreciably. As these changes in behavior became more pronounced, I feared for what might happen next. I wanted to know what could be done to reduce the anxiety and agitation she was experiencing.

In mid-October, I asked for another meeting with the same Covenant Memory Care staff. They were happy to agree because they had similar concerns about Sally's behavior. We reviewed Sally's records to decide what to do. It was at this time, when presented with a full accounting of Sally's aberrant—even abusive—actions, that I first became aware of the full extent of her disruptive behavior. I was startled to be confronted with three full pages of nursing case notes detailing multiple incidents of hostility and aggression.

The nurse manager and social worker concluded that Sally needed an antipsychotic medication to calm her agitation and anxiety. They recommended Seroquel, a drug that they were quite familiar with and had used with a number of Covenant residents. I told the nurse manager to proceed with her plan to calm Sally's behavior with Seroquel. At the same time, I realized I knew nothing about antipsychotic medications, much less Seroquel, a medication I had never heard of before.

The Communication Problem

The nurse manager said she would that she would immediately contact Sally's primary care doctor that afternoon to see if he would prescribe Seroquel. At that same meeting, the staff informed me that if Sally's agitation and anxiety became a threat to herself or to other residents and staff, and if she could not be calmed down, their policy required that she be sent to a hospital emergency room. I did not give much thought to this possibility, assuming the antipsychotic medication would become available quickly and do its work.

Several days later, I spoke with the nurse manager about the status of her request, and she told me she had been phoning Sally's doctor regularly, but his line was always busy, or he was unavailable. She had to leave several messages for him to return her calls. When he did return her calls, *she* was always busy and could not talk to him. Their attempts over the next week never led to their speaking directly to one another. I was surprised no better method of communication existed between doctors and nurses.

As a result, Sally remained without the medication the Covenant staff believed would bring her agitation and anxiety under control. The more than weeklong delay already had serious consequences. In fact, this proved to be the first of a string of communication lapses over the next several weeks. I was not happy with the situation. Rather than getting angry, however, it led me to think about how to improve communication between the memory-care nurse and the primary care doctor, and more generally among health care personnel at different kinds and levels of care. Following several additional moves for Sally, I compiled a list of these suggestions. (They can be found in a later chapter.)

As a consequence of this continuing communication breakdown, Sally, now an eighty-four-year-old woman with no acute physical health problems, was transported to the UW Hospital for three emergency room visits. This was followed by two hospital stays that totaled nineteen days in addition to a four-day stay in a skilled nursing home, sandwiched between the two hospital stays. Not until she was well into her second hospitalization did the UW Hospital initiate the antipsychotic medication regimen the Covenant nurse had requested. This occurred only after my several phone calls and letters to Sally's doctor, discussions with numerous UW Hospital doctors, and a telephone conference with our two daughters, the attending UW Hospital doctor, and Sally's associated social worker.

On an Antipsychotic Medication

Immediately after that seminal meeting with the Covenant staff, I realized I needed to know more about Seroquel and its effects. I spoke with the Oakwood pharmacist who told me about the Food and Drug Administration's black box warnings about its side effects, particularly with elderly people suffering from dementia. He also told me that though Seroquel was administered to a number of Covenant residents, he and his colleagues regularly checked on its use and tried to minimize it. He provided me with a most helpful copy of a National Institute of Aging book about caring for people with dementia, the widely distributed National Institute for Aging (NIA) report *Caring for a Person with Alzheimer's Disease: Your Easy-to-Use Guide from the National Institute for Aging*. (Publication No. 12-6173, March 2010. Updated May 2013).

I soon discovered that the reporting of Seroquel's side effects was deficient and completely ignored its beneficial effects in improving the quality of life. (What I learned is described in a later chapter.)

I then asked the Oakwood pharmacist his opinion on whether Seroquel would be an appropriate medication for Sally in her circumstances. He thought it would be helpful in the short run, but he also alerted me to its serious side effects. When I pushed for more detail on these adverse effects, he directed me to the research literature where I learned much more.

The side effects included the increased risk of stroke, heart failure, irregular heartbeat, pneumonia, the increased possibility of falling, and even death. The black box warning, based on clinical trials, demonstrated that for the elderly with dementia, the risk of death from taking Seroquel was between 1.6 to 1.7 times greater than for those taking the placebo. Because the FDA believed this risk was too high, it issued a warning that Seroquel should not be administered to the elderly, particularly to those who suffered from dementia psychosis.

None of these apparently serious side effects had been mentioned at the meeting with Sally's care team. My quick review of the NIA report that the pharmacist had given me indicated that the risks of Seroquel needed to be balanced off against its benefits of improving the quality of life for people suffering from dementia-related agitation and anxiety. Oddly, there was no explicit mention of these possible benefits.

What I soon learned after Sally's hospitalization following her second emergency room visit is that health care professionals working with elderly people suffering from severe dementia seemed to be unduly influenced by the FDA's black box warnings on antipsychotic medications such as Seroquel, including Risperdal and Zyprexa. In my subsequent discussions with physicians about using these drugs to help elderly dementia patients such as my wife, they consistently mentioned the heightened risk of death, but again, they rarely mentioned the beneficial effects of Seroquel on a patient's quality of life. This heightened concern about the risks of Seroquel later showed up on the discharge papers from her first hospital stay in November 2013.

Had I been asked by UW Hospital personnel whether Sally should be given Seroquel to treat her agitation, I would have answered with an emphatic "yes." It seemed to me that the benefits to her comfort far outweighed the risk factors. But was I asked? No, I was not. Nor did I know enough about patient rights and my rights as Sally's durable power of attorney for health care to contest the decision to withhold Seroquel.

On Seroquel's Risks

The administration of Seroquel to memory-care residents was not that unusual. At the memory-care unit where Sally resided, the pharmacist informed me that as many as 20 percent of the residents received this drug.

Caring for a Person with Alzheimer's Disease: Your Easy-to-Use Guide from the National Institute for Aging contains a discussion of antipsychotic medications for people with dementia and touches briefly on the risk question in a section entitled "Medications to be Used with Caution." Page 76 reads: "Anti-psychotics are drugs used to treat paranoia, hallucinations, agitation, and aggression ... Side effects of using these drugs can be serious, including increased risk of death in some older people with dementia. They should only be given to people with AD (Alzheimer's disease) when the doctor agrees that the symptoms are severe."

It struck me as odd that this important and widely distributed publication was so vague about the risks that are the subject of the FDA black box warning. This discovery led me to intensify my search for information about these risk factors. The most obvious place to look was the Medication Guide that is included in packages of Seroquel. After unfolding the folded instruction sheet, I located its Frequently Asked Questions section that opened with the question: "What is the most important information I should know?" It says this: "Risk of death in the elderly with dementia. Medicines like quetiapine Fumarate tablets can increase the risk of death in elderly people who have memory loss (dementia). Quetiapine fumarate tablets are not approved for treating psychosis in the elderly with dementia."

Because nothing more is said in the Medication Guide about the magnitude of the risk factor, I checked the single-page Patient Information Leaflet Quetiapine - ORAL. This sheet is given out with filled prescriptions when people obtain Seroquel prescriptions through their pharmacy. The opening paragraph reads: "WARNING: There may be a slightly increased risk of serious, possibly fatal side effects (such as stroke, heart failure, fast/irregular heartbeat, pneumonia) when this medication is used by older adults with dementia."

There is no further elaboration. The phrases "slightly increased risk" and "possible fatal side effects" struck me as only mildly informative and hardly appropriate considering the substantial risk factor of 60–70 percent mentioned by several doctors who had visited Sally while she was hospitalized.

The FDA Warning

The full text of the risk warning issued by the FDA can be read on the internet by googling "FDA black box warning Seroquel." Analyses of 17 placebo-controlled trials (modal duration of 10 weeks), largely in patients taking atypical antipsychotic drugs, reveal a risk of death in the drug-treated patients between 1.6 to 1.7 times that seen in placebo-treated patients ... " (Note: "atypical" refers to second generation drugs that have reduced side effects.)

So at last, this was the source of the information about the hazards of using Seroquel. However, there is more to the warning than indicated in the warning's first paragraph. It goes on to include important information that seems to have been largely ignored by the health care professionals I encountered. The rest of the warning reads: "Over the course of a typical 10-week controlled trial, the rate of death in drug-treated patients was about 4.5 percent compared with a rate of about 2.6 percent in the placebo group."

While the large 1.6 to 1.7 increased risk of death sounds ominous, the death rate for those being treated is still low because of the small baseline rate of 2.6 percent. Even with the 4.5 percent death rate, 95.5 percent of the treated group apparently experienced none of the mentioned side effects.

The paragraph continues: "Although the causes of death were varied, most of the deaths appeared to be either cardiovascular (e.g., heart failure, sudden death) or infectious (e.g., pneumonia) in nature. Observational studies suggest that, similar to other antipsychotic drugs, treatment with conventional atypical antipsychotic drugs may increase mortality. The extent to which the findings of increased mortality in observational studies may be attributed to the antipsychotic drug as opposed to some characteristic(s) of the patients is not clear."

My reading of the above paragraph suggests that the causes of the reported deaths could have been attributed to "some characteristics of the patients" rather than Seroquel. The paragraph concludes with the following sentence: "Seroquel is not approved for the treatment of patients with dementia-related psychosis (see WARNINGS)."

In my estimation, this somewhat higher death rate associated with Seroquel is not sufficiently greater to be unacceptable. I say this because

I later witnessed the antipsychotic drug's power to greatly reduce Sally's agitation and aggression. It also eliminated her paranoid and hallucinatory behaviors, which were much less frequent though they certainly merited attention. Moreover, starting her on Seroquel to cope with her immediate symptoms did not mean she would receive this medication in perpetuity.

When health care personnel speak about the risks of antipsychotic drugs, including the dire possibilities of heart attacks, strokes, pneumonia, and even death, patients and their caregivers are bound to pay close attention. But should they not press for more detail? In my opinion, they should.

Risks versus Benefits

Health care personnel should be required to discuss with patients and their families these risks along with the benefits of Seroquel. Patients and their families should also know that because of the low baseline death rate, the seemingly large percentage increase in the risk of death does not translate into a prohibitively high death rate.

We are left with the tradeoff posed by the following question: For dementia sufferers who are given Seroquel to reduce their dementia-related agitation and anxiety, how does their increased comfort and quality of life stack up against the heightened risk of death?

Again, much too little is said about the benefits of Seroquel in a case like Sally's. The drug manufacturer does mention in its literature on this medication that "All medications have risks and benefits." It continues: "Your doctor will have weighed the risks of your taking Seroquel against the benefits they expect it will have for you." This statement may be comforting but is hardly satisfactory in view of the absolute prohibition in the FDA warning, namely that Seroquel should not be used in "the treatment of patients with dementia-related psychosis."[1]

The medical profession's commitment to save and extend people's lives ignores the understandable interest that people, including a growing number

1 The current Medication Guide for Seroquel, described as approved by the U.S. Food and Drug Administration (Seroquel 020639s061,022047s034lbl, downloaded June 20, 2010), mentions that Seroquel can increase the risk of death in elderly people with dementia. But the extent of the risk contained in the FDA black box warning is nowhere to be found.

of doctors, have in improving the quality of life for elderly family members who suffer from severe dementia. In Sally's case, antipsychotic drugs, by reducing or eliminating anxiety, agitation, paranoia, and hallucinations, substantially improved the quality of her life. The health care system should be focusing on how to do this for all elderly who suffer from advanced dementia.

The problem was finally resolved after a clarifying telephone conference call among the UW Hospital doctor, the social worker, me, and our two out-of-town daughters. The presiding doctor during Sally's second hospitalization seemed reluctant to put Sally on Seroquel until this conference call. The call took place on the fourth full day of Sally's second hospitalization, and it focused heavily on the extent of the family's prior discussions with Sally about what kind of end-of-life medical care she wanted if dementia overtook her. She clearly wanted "death with dignity," leading to a quick and painless death.

The doctor was convinced. As soon as Sally was given the appropriate dosage of Seroquel, her agitation and anxiety subsided and remained that way for the following months.

What If ... ?

What if, in October 2013, when Sally's agitation and aggressive behavior increased sharply, it had been possible to immediately begin administering Seroquel? While the outcome is impossible to predict, it seems likely that Sally's three trips to the ER brought on by her extreme states of agitation and her subsequent hospitalizations would not have been necessary. Indeed, she might have continued living in Covenant Oaks Memory Care unit where she initially lived instead of having to be transferred elsewhere. The considerable anguish suffered by Sally, my two daughters, and me could have been avoided.

What is my explanation for what happened beginning with Sally's second ER visit that led to her first hospitalization? I believe it goes back to Sally's history of depression and the two severe bouts of it that she experienced in the fall of 2010 and spring of 2012. Based on her medical records, it appears that her primary care doctor, the UW Hospital Emergency Room medical teams, and Sally's attending doctors at UW Hospital all treated her as someone who was once again depressed.

This treatment may have been appropriate to the extent that she could have become depressed after being moved to the Covenant Oaks Memory Care unit. There are other reasons that made treating her for depression understandable. I have been told that distinguishing between depression with psychotic features and the psychotic symptoms of dementia can be difficult, especially in patients with a history of depression or prominent negative symptoms.

What is different about Sally's case is that the staff at Covenant Memory Care had been able to observe her behavior directly over the previous several months. They had ample time to observe her prominent symptoms of heightened agitation and anxiety. Even if Sally had been taken for an appointment with her primary care doctor, it is not clear what kind of diagnosis would have emerged because of the customary short appointment times allotted for patient office visits. With Sally's well-developed social skills, she could have easily concealed her true condition; this is something she had been able to do in previous visits with her primary care doctor. Regarding her subsequent hospitalizations, the same question could be asked about the accuracy of the diagnoses made by hospital doctors during their brief visits with her while making their morning rounds.

In retrospect, this much is clear: Ample evidence indicating the full extent of Sally's agitation and anxiety did not get communicated to her personal physician. That evidence was contained in her memory-care records and earlier medical records, as well as my firsthand reports of her behavior that I conveyed by letter and phone conversation to her primary care doctor, to ER doctors, and UW Hospital doctors. Unfortunately, my direct knowledge of her agitation and anxiety failed to register with any of them until well into her second hospitalization. By then, it had become clear that treating Sally for depression failed to produce the improvement her personal doctor and the UW Hospital staff had hoped for, as indicated by her hospitalization discharge record.

When qualified health care personnel directly observe the behavior of patients, they develop a body of valuable information. There must be better ways of communicating this information and making sure it's not ignored.

The widely touted, adverse side effects of Seroquel never touched Sally despite the long duration of time that she took the medication. Who knows how the course of her life might have played out had Seroquel become available to her while she was still at Oakwood's Covenant Oaks Memory Care?

Sally's Five Wishes

During these several weeks of turmoil, I forgot about Sally's lack of concern about the risks of medication she might be given. In fact, Sally's witnessed "Five Wishes" document, dated December 16, 2012, shown in the section "WISH 1: What You Should Keep in Mind As My Caregiver" stated "I do not want to be in pain. I want my doctor to give me enough medicine to relieve my pain, even if that means that I will be drowsy or sleep more than I otherwise would." Sally had then written "OR THAT IT MIGHT HASTEN MY DEATH." In the section "WISH 3: My Wish for How Comfortable I want to BE," she stated "I do not want to be in pain. I want my doctor to give me enough medicine to relieve any pain, even if that means I will be drowsy or sleep more than I otherwise would," after which she wrote "AND EVEN IF IT HASTENS MY DEATH." Unfortunately, I was too preoccupied with Sally's more immediate needs to recall what she had written. Nor was I carrying this and related end-of-life documents to show to the health care professionals taking care of her. Nor did I think of asking the attending health professionals to examine their medical records for her Five Wishes document, which I had earlier deposited at the UW Hospital. What weight her additional statements might have carried with the hospital staff remains unclear.

Chapter 6

CHAOS

The Beginning

The sun shone on the turning leaves on that late October afternoon as I headed to visit Sally at Covenant Oaks. I expected to find her doing what I usually found her doing, walking up and down the corridors assisted by her walker. I attributed this activity to her dementia-induced agitation. As well, it gave her something to do. This time, she sat on a chair planted directly in front of the closed door to her room. When I asked why she was sitting there, she expressed the fear somebody might come and steal her possessions, particularly the portrait of her and her cat, Ivan, which hung above her bed. I wondered where she had gotten this idea. I reassured her that nothing like that could happen, but she was not persuaded. At that point, I had to leave briefly for an appointment with the nurse to discuss Sally's medications.

When I returned an hour later, dinner was being served. Sally remained seated in her chair outside her room. Her door remained locked. She explained again she wanted to prevent someone from entering her room and stealing her paintings. I tried to convince her to join me for dinner. Although she finally agreed, she insisted we sit a table that allowed her to watch her door. Such paranoid behavior, I learned later, is not uncommon for people suffering from dementia. Their behavior should not be surprising. With so much loss and change, can we blame her or others for their attachments and paranoia? Wasn't everything being taken from her? Her past? Her home? Her hope? No wonder she wanted to die. Sitting guard over what she had left may not be as crazy as it appears to those who still have all of their possessions.

After we finished dinner, Sally asked what I had done that day. I told her I had visited the UW Archives to look up some information about the Economics Department. At that time in her progression of dementia she still showed some interest in my life. Later, I took her to her room to help her get ready for bed. As I had occasionally done for the past months that she lived in Memory Care, I slipped off her clothes and placed them on her favored chair, one that was a family heirloom. By then she was no longer concerned about losing her coveted cat painting. After that night Sally never sat on guard again.

Sally's room held many beloved possessions, which included a book of large photographs revealing the deterioration of Detroit, Michigan, where she grew up, several books on literature and poetry, and two paintings by her uncle of the Saugatuck, Michigan, area where she had spent many summers while growing up. An abundance of family photographs was posted on a white board I had purchased for her. A favorite reading lamp that she still used intermittently sat on the table near her bed. That table, made of black walnut, was a family heirloom of mine that she liked. She had no need before or then for a television.

More Aggression

That week continued to be rough for Sally. She became more aggressive in her interactions with other residents. From time to time she blocked their progress in the hallways with her walker. That Saturday, our daughter, Ellen, drove up from Glen Ellyn, Illinois, to visit her mother, arriving about mid-morning. Having been travelling for the past several weeks, she simply wanted to see her mother even though Sally no longer recognized her. Of course, Sally's increasing memory loss created a larger and larger distance between them. Those suffering from dementia do not recognize the gap as much as those on the other side seeking a connection do. I found this progression sad. I, too, carried the same burden of fond memories that Sally was quickly losing.

On our arrival, a resident attendant told us that Sally had been in a foul mood ever since getting up that morning, among other things cursing at staff members trying to help her. When Ellen greeted Sally, Sally refused to talk to her. Sally also refused to speak with me. The gap was getting larger and larger. After repeated failures to engage with her, Ellen and I decided to shop for some clothes Sally needed and have lunch together. We both were sad and mystified by Sally's lack of interest in talking with us. She had so loved long conversations.

On our return, we learned that Sally had been entering the rooms of other residents, using their bathrooms, and acting generally obnoxious. Because Sally continued her silence, Ellen gave up and decided to return home. My grief was doubled when I witnessed my adult children suffer through their mother's decline. I remained with Sally. I wanted to figure out what bothered her.

The most obvious possibility was a worsening of her dementia. She may have been rebelling against living in such a restricted environment of memory care after enjoying nearly a half-century in our spacious home. Still another possibility—she was trying to get even with me for transferring her to Covenant Memory Care several months earlier. All three explanations may have been intertwined, but this type of speculation rarely took me anywhere helpful. Her behavior would continue to puzzle me. As I returned to my nearby apartment for supper, I continued to speculate. More important, I couldn't help but wonder whether her behavior was a prelude to what would come. Of course, I soon found out.

Emergency Room Care

On the following Monday, Sally had her first trip to the UW Hospital Emergency Room. The day started with a 5:30 a.m. phone call from one of the Covenant Oaks resident assistants.

"Mr. Hansen? Can you come over here? We really need your help in dealing with Sally's behavior," she asked. I dressed and hurried over, but Sally was not in her room. When I found her, she was sitting in a chair in another resident's room. That resident, still lying on his bed, was upset about Sally's invasion, yelling at her to leave. I then noticed blood dripping on the floor from Sally's wrist. A closer look indicated that the bandage covering a skin tear from a recent fall was half torn off.

The resident assistant told me she and her colleagues had been unable to convince Sally to leave the resident's room. I tried to convince Sally to get up and sit in a wheelchair, but she categorically refused. When I grasped her upper arm to move her, she tried to hit me. After she calmed down a bit, the resident assistant and I quickly lifted Sally by her arms, hoisting her into her wheelchair. I then wheeled her back to her room. When the LPN arrived and attempted to take her vital signs and clean and bandage her wound, Sally refused to allow her to proceed.

It was uncomfortable to see someone I loved behaving in such an odd fashion. Though still my wife, she acted like a stranger, doing things that were completely out of character. She had become a person who looked like my Sally but was acting like someone no one would associate with. I likened this to a caregiver's dilemma of tending to someone who is no longer themselves and is often resistant or too angry to help.

With Sally's refusal, the LPN said she would have to contact her supervisor about sending Sally to a hospital ER because of safety concerns, possible injuries, and a bloody and unattended wound that could become infected. An ambulance arrived about twenty minutes later. The two ambulance attendants told Sally they had come to take her to the ER and needed to help her onto the gurney they'd brought with them. She refused to allow them to help her out of the wheelchair and onto the gurney. I joined in trying unsuccessfully to get Sally to cooperate. When the attendants attempted to humor her by saying the ride to the hospital would only take about fifteen minutes, she suggested they all walk there! On hearing her response, I was embarrassed.

After more verbal sparring, Sally finally allowed them to help her stand up so she could be maneuvered to sit on the gurney. Then she refused to allow them to lift her legs onto it. Following an additional five-minute delay, she complied. With that, the ambulance drove her off to the UW Hospital Emergency Room.

On her arrival, the usual blood and urine tests were conducted. X-rays were taken of Sally's hand, arm, and hip. A CT scan was taken of her head to check for injuries she might have incurred in falls two nights earlier. I was questioned about Sally and explained that she was suffering from dementia and needed an antipsychotic medication for her anxiety and agitation, but nobody seemed to pay any attention to what I said. Shortly afterward, I was relieved to learn that the results of the tests and x-rays were all negative. In fact, several ER staff members remarked about how fit Sally was. Her arm wound was treated and bandaged, and she was sent by ambulance back to Covenant Oaks.

Primary Care Doctor Contact

At this point, Sally was not yet on Seroquel. En route to the ER that morning, I had stopped at my apartment to pick up a letter I had written the previous evening to Sally's primary care doctor. That letter described Sally's increased agitation and erratic behavior, including several of the already mentioned events of the previous week. I suggested that she needed an antipsychotic drug, such as Seroquel, to calm her down and enable her to live a more normal life at Covenant Oaks. I also pointed out his lack of communication with the Covenant Oaks nurse. Because the letter was too long to send to her primary care doctor via Sally's electronic UW Health My Chart account, I left a copy at the doctor's office. I hoped my letter would spur him to prescribe the Seroquel medication Sally so desperately needed.

Late that afternoon, Sally's primary care doctor surprised me with a phone call at my apartment. Rather than prescribing an antipsychotic drug as I hoped he would do, he said the dosage of Sally's Prozac, a medication she had been using for many years to combat depression, should be doubled from 10 to 20 mg. Despite the evidence presented in my letter and his prior knowledge of Sally's dementia, he apparently attributed her erratic behavior to depression. I was too surprised to object. I did recall later reading in a medical journal about, as mentioned previously, the difficulty of distinguishing between the symptoms of dementia and depression. Perhaps this was the problem or contributing to it.

The next afternoon, the Covenant case nurse asked me to approve the new prescription. She suggested the 20 mg dosage might not be enough. That seemed like a good idea. Before signing the authorization form, I raised the maximum dosage to 40 mg. At this point, I was beginning to question the quality of care Sally was receiving. If she needed more Prozac, I wanted the doctors to have ample flexibility to administer a stronger dosage.

The Days Ahead

The next day, I was back at Covenant Oaks and on edge. I was apprehensive about Sally's behavior. Though she smiled more readily and was more civil in her relations with other residents and staff, she was still anxious and somewhat agitated. The following day, I received another frantic phone call from the staff, this time in mid-morning. Sally was again highly agitated, using her walker to obstruct other residents walking in the corridors. She also blocked the preschool children brought to Covenant to participate in a Halloween event to "trick or treat" the "grandmas and grandpas." Her behavior was so aggressive toward the trick-or-treaters that staff members actually formed a human barrier to keep her from threatening the children as well as other residents. Because the staff regarded her as constituting a threat to herself, the staff, and the visiting preschool kids, Sally was again, based on Covenant's Memory Care policy, sent by ambulance to the UW Hospital ER for treatment.

What had happened that morning surprised me because Sally especially enjoyed Halloween. She regularly bought a good stock of chocolate to dispense to the 100 or so little kids who regularly appeared at our door in search of treats. She always made sure some of the chocolates remained for us to snack on over the next couple of days.

At the Hospital

When I arrived at the brightly lit ER, Sally was still highly agitated, angry, and uncooperative. She refused to allow her vital signs to be taken or to be examined by the ER staff.

Upon seeing me, she grabbed me and yet again asked me to assist in her demise. I had to try and comfort her as best I could until she was given a strong sedative and drifted off to sleep, enabling the staff to attend to her.

To the best of my knowledge, her Prozac dosage had not yet been increased the day before, and this may have accounted in part for Sally's behavior that morning. Nobody could explain why her medication was not increased the previous evening. Later I learned it had not been delivered in time for its bedtime administration. This breakdown may or may not have had much effect on Sally's behavior. Still, it was too bad she was not awakened and given her increased dose of Prozac. Following considerable consultation with ER staff and several hospital doctors that evening, I agreed with their decision to admit Sally to the hospital's geriatric unit for observation and treatment. The next morning, they increased her Prozac dosage to 40 mg. She had also been given Trazodone the night before to help her sleep, and according to reports from the nurses, it proved to be highly effective.

At this time, the UW Hospital happened to be engaged in an aggressive program to prevent patients from falling. Because of her history of falling and fainting, a round-the-clock "watcher" was assigned to Sally's room to make certain she did not attempt to get out of bed on her own. Sally could well have interpreted the presence of the watcher as a guard to restrict her freedom of movement even more. What can be reassuring for staff and family can be interpreted as threat or hindrance to those with dementia. But how can we ever truly know what is in another's mind and experience? We can't. The caretakers and the ones suffering dementia live in parallel worlds—worlds that tend to collide.

Over the next few days, I spent much of my time at the hospital trying to find out what treatment Sally received. One day two young geriatric doctors stopped by at different times to find out more about my wife. In response to my expressed concern about Sally's need for an antipsychotic medication to deal with her continued agitation, each of them mentioned the FDA's black box warnings about the adverse side effects of Seroquel, among them heart problems, strokes, pneumonia, and even death. Though I argued her immediate comfort and well-being were more important than these long-term risks, I made no headway with either of them. Seroquel's side effect of possible death was not of great concern to me in view of Sally's belief in her right to die. In retrospect, I should have been more forceful in making my case.

During her weeklong hospital stay, Sally remained calm, displaying neither agitation nor anxiety. Everyone on the hospital staff felt she had improved. Was her agitated state now a thing of the past? It seemed so, but I was dubious. I believed her improved behavior more likely resulted from the calming medications she'd received. A week passed, and after their evaluation, the medical staff believed Sally should be discharged.

A Brief Stay in Skilled Nursing

Because Sally now needed assistance to stand and get to the toilet, the Covenant Oaks Memory Care staff informed me that she would not be allowed to return there. Its staff could not provide the level of care Sally required. This news was terribly disappointing. What would I do now? Fortunately, I soon realized there was another place to send her, namely Hebron Oaks, the skilled nursing care unit maintained by Oakwood Village. The Covenant Oaks nurse manager and members of the Hebron Oaks skilled nursing staff visited the UW Hospital twice to evaluate Sally for a move to Hebron, and a decision was finally made to admit her. A day or so later she was transported there by ambulance. This time, because of her continued sedation, Sally was in no shape to object to this move.

Sally's stay in the skilled nursing care unit was brief. On her first full day she was fine. The next day she became highly agitated. Then she had another good day that included a visit by a couple of old friends from Oakwood Village, but in the mid-afternoon of her fourth day there, I received another phone call telling me that Sally was rolling her wheelchair into the rooms of other patients, objecting when residents refused to let her into their apartments, and using foul language to both residents and staff members. I now realized the increased dosage of Prozac and her weeklong hospital stay produced no lasting effect in reducing her agitation and anxiety.

Back to UW Hospital

That Sunday afternoon, Sally was sent back to the UW Hospital ER for a third time. On this occasion, she was even more agitated than during her previous ER visits, objecting to everything the ER staff tried to do. To calm her down, she was injected with Ativan and Haldol. When the ER staff asked for background information on Sally, I explained her need for an antipsychotic drug to deal with the agitated behavior they were presently witnessing.

Several doctors came to examine her, including the doctor that subsequently took charge of her care during her ensuing second hospitalization. Though I spoke with the doctors to explain why Sally was the way she was—it was because of her dementia—they did not respond. It seemed as if they thought the knowledge of a spouse could not be relied upon in a situation like this. How unprofessional to reject the information from me who cared for Sally for so long and from Sally's medical record that presumably contained the two letters I had submitted to her personal physician. It was very distressing.

Later that afternoon, Sally was readmitted to the UW Hospital for observation and additional treatment during what became a ten-day stay. Again, a person was assigned to watch Sally on a twenty-four-hour basis to ensure she did not try to get out of bed and fall.

I remained convinced that Sally needed antipsychotic medication to deal with her agitation and anxiety. Following talks with the Oakwood pharmacist after the Covenant nurse had recommended Seroquel some weeks earlier, I began reading some of the literature on Seroquel and became less awed by the claims made about its adverse side effects, particularly the increased likelihood of death. Though the death rate for these older people getting Seroquel in the clinical trials increased substantially, it did so from such a low base that the higher death rate remained quite low.

Seroquel is what the Memory Care staff at Oakwood Village had hoped Sally's primary care doctor would prescribe, and this is what I had recommended to him in the letters I'd delivered to his office. This is also what I suggested to the doctors during her first hospital stay. However, her primary care doctor and a geriatric doctor he consulted as well as the attending hospital physicians—including the two geriatric specialists—were all reluctant to prescribe what seemed to me to be a much-needed antipsychotic.

The doctors continued to justify their decision by referring to the risks detailed in the FDA black box warnings for antipsychotic drugs and the possible adverse side effects of these drugs, including death. Again, I argued that Sally's immediate comfort and well-being were more important than the small and unlikely long-term risks. My pleas continued to fall on deaf ears. How discouraging.

I wondered why the earlier Covenant Oaks Memory Care's recommendation of Seroquel did not factor into their consideration. I suspect it was because antipsychotics had a long history of overuse in nursing homes, where efforts to keep residents "calm" resulted in overmedication and sedation. This past history of abuse very likely became another reason for the reluctance of the hospital staff to prescribe an antipsychotic for Sally. Whatever the reasons, I found it extremely frustrating that nobody seemed willing to listen to my views or to consider the Covenant recommendation.

During Sally's third ER visit, I again urged the ER staff to give Sally an antipsychotic medication. The next morning, I dropped off another letter to Sally's primary care doctor, updating him on Sally's agitation and anxiety. I repeated my request that he prescribe the antipsychotic drug, Seroquel, as recommended by the Covenant Oaks staff, to deal with her condition. I also gave a copy of this letter to the UW Hospital doctor supervising Sally's care, and I discussed with her Sally's need for an antipsychotic drug. She listened to me, but she made no mention of the black box warning.

Later that afternoon while napping at home, I received another phone call from Sally's primary care doctor. In response to my second letter, he agreed that Sally needed an antipsychotic drug. By this time, he may have had an opportunity to review the sheaf of case notes faxed to him several weeks earlier by Covenant's Memory Care unit nurse manager. I don't recall whether or how he said he would convey his recommendation to the hospital staff.

Taking a Stand

The next morning, with heightened concern and frustration, I pressed the doctor for Sally to get an antipsychotic. I told the hospital doctor and social worker involved in Sally's care that we needed to resolve what medication should be given to Sally. Our two daughters would be involved via a telephone conference. Meanwhile, the hospital doctor, unbeknownst to me, finally decided to start Sally on a low dose of Seroquel. Later, I learned from the hospital doctor that Sally's primary care doctor did not pass on his recommendation to the hospital doctor, nor did the hospital doctor contact Sally's primary care doctor about her decision to start Sally on Seroquel. A copy of my second letter to Sally's primary care doctor that I gave to the

UW Hospital doctor may have convinced her to start Sally on the minimum dose of Seroquel. What most distressed me was the lack of communication between the two medical doctors.

Two days later, we had the phone conference that included the doctor, social worker, and our two daughters. I submitted a background statement describing Sally's wish that no heroic measures be taken to prolong her life as well as our belief she should be given an antipsychotic drug because the quality-of-life benefits would vastly outweigh the increased risk of adverse side effects. This statement was consistent with my ongoing battle to see that she was given Seroquel. The increased risk of death from Seroquel which might accelerate her death was also consistent with Sally's belief in her right to die.

The conference began with the doctor's succinct summary of Sally's condition, adding that in her estimation, Sally's dementia was progressing rapidly, as revealed by the marked increase in her agitated behavior and the loss of her ability to walk. (I was not certain about the accuracy of the doctor's statement about Sally's legs. I thought the concern about her legs was related to the UW Hospital's program to reduce falls, something more likely to occur in a strange environment.) We then brought up the need for an antipsychotic medication to reduce her agitation, pain, and confusion. We explained why we were not concerned with the risks associated with Seroquel.

We made it clear that Sally and I, along with our daughters, had engaged in extensive conversations in the past about end-of-life issues. Our daughters had seen our Estate Plan with its end-of-life provisions. They had been present during our numerous dinner table conversations about end-of-life issues.

Based on Sally's long and strongly held view favoring assisted suicide and her belief in a demented individual's right to die, I said that Sally's condition had already deteriorated well beyond what she would want it to be. Indeed, she had often expressed aloud her desire to die, asking me to help her do so. I added that if she could voice her feelings on the matter, she would agree that the Seroquel medication should be administered, even with its small risk of a shortened lifespan. The family made it clear we all agreed Sally should receive only palliative (i.e., comfort) care. We were not advocating any hastening of Sally's death, but neither did we wish to prolong her life in her current condition, which if she could choose, she would choose to end.

The hospital doctor was sympathetic to our collective wish to avoid any heroic measures and to make sure that Sally be made as comfortable as possible in the time that remained to her. Her answer was exactly what we wanted to hear. We knew too many people who suffered because they had no way to release themselves from life.

During this meeting, the doctor wiped away a tear or two. Perplexed by this, I later asked her about her tears. She told me she had been moved emotionally by the phone conference. Not only were Ellen, Martha, and I in complete agreement about what needed to be done, but the basis for that agreement rested on our prior discussions with Sally. The doctor explained that frequently this was not the case in end-of-life situations. In fact, she said there was often substantial disagreement among family members about what should be done. She was both relieved and moved by our ability to demonstrate consensus in this difficult situation.

This experience strengthened our already strong belief that all families should spend time talking about how they want to be cared for at the end of their lives. The subject is not as difficult to talk about as so many people fear. There are now also numerous books and pamphlets available to help families do this.

Success at Last

We then came to an agreement that the hospital staff would immediately accelerate its administration of Seroquel. The plan called for increasing its dosage until it seemed to be taking effect. The initial dose had been 12.5 mg. in the morning, at noon, and at bedtime. That dosage was immediately increased to 25 mg. in the morning and 50 mg. at noon and again at bedtime. By the following Sunday, three days later, Sally's agitation had completely subsided. To think how Sally's life would have differed if Seroquel had been made available to her when it was first recommended by the Covenant nurse or during her first hospitalization almost two weeks earlier!

Both the doctor and the social worker thought that Sally needed to be moved to a quiet environment. They believed the most appropriate placement would be the residential unit of the local Agrace Hospice Care. I believe their decision was at least partially driven by their concern about the difficulty of my quickly finding another nursing home for Sally.

Because my wife had already been hospitalized for more than a week and the medication seemed to be working, the hospital staff was under pressure to release her. The following Monday, the hospital social worker informed me she had already checked and learned that neither the Covenant Memory Care nor Hebron, the skilled nursing unit at Oakwood Village, would readmit Sally.

Later that day, I received a confirming letter from the Oakwood Village administration saying, "Our team is strongly recommending a geriatric psych referral and treatment before reassessing to see if Oakwood could meet her needs." The letter suggested a possible referral to an apparently well-regarded geriatric psychiatry inpatient program in Stoughton, Wisconsin. For me, this was a nonstarter. I knew that such an evaluation would take considerable time and expense. I also realized that the record of Sally's behavior would bias any decision to readmit her to Covenant Memory Care.

Chapter 7

RELIEF

THE NEXT MORNING, I ate breakfast and then drank my morning coffee while watching the birds feasting at the bird feeder mounted outside my fifth-floor window. After Sally had retired, she'd taken a keener interest in birds and their behavior. She and I had often spent similar moments together back at our Topping Road home before beginning our day's activities. Now I realized there would be no more such moments for the two of us. Not only was Sally no longer the person she once was, but she was unlikely ever to return with me to the life-lease apartment I occupied.

A phone call shortly after 9:00 a.m. interrupted my reveries. The call came from Agrace Hospice Care informing me that Sally had been admitted and could be moved in immediately. All my worry over the weekend had been for naught.

Sally's Move to Agrace

I made immediate arrangements for her transfer. Two days later, an ambulance transported Sally from UW Hospital to Agrace. After observation, they moved her to a room in its residential care section where she began an extended stay. I was pleased to know Sally was now in the lovely facility where she would receive the quality care Agrace was so well known for.

Though Sally was not in end-of-life care, I realized her decline would continue, and eventually, she would die at Agrace. I suppose this was a natural assumption that family members would make about anyone moved to residential hospice care. If the hospital doctor's prediction was correct, Sally might live for another two to two and a half years. How accurate that prediction might be was anyone's guess.

As soon as friends heard Sally now lived at Agrace, they worried she might be terminal. I put their minds at ease when I explained that she had been moved to the residential section where she could live in a quiet, restful environment that would reduce the agitation and anxiety she experienced in Covenant Memory Care.

After Sally moved to Agrace, every effort was made to ensure she did not fall, with alarms installed in her bed and wheelchair and large rubber pads on both sides of her bed. When on one or two occasions she tried to get up, nurses came flying into the room to tuck her back into bed. As a caregiver, you should insist on these precautions; a fall for older people can often have serious, even fatal implications.

Another concern that may arise for a loved one, as it did for Sally, was incontinence. This led the staff to install a catheter. Shortly after doing so, Sally pulled it out. Following several more attempts, the staff recognized Sally would always have to be assisted when going to the toilet. That had already been the case at the UW Hospital and also at Covenant Oaks Memory Care.

If you're a caregiver, I hope you will do what I did when Sally arrived at Agrace. I made it abundantly clear that she did not want any efforts made to extend her life. Make certain your loved one's chart includes this important information. If that is the wish of your loved one, remember to provide the caregiving staff with any and all end-of-life documents that describe how your loved one wants to be treated in their final days. The staff assured me they would honor her request.

Some Peace

Sally's agitation and anxiety remained under control with the help of Seroquel. However, she was no longer the Sally she had been even a few months earlier. Although in fair spirits, she appeared to be in a "fog" much of the time. She was not always certain who I was, she experienced difficulty expressing herself, and she seemed to be increasingly preoccupied with her thoughts. The Agrace staff attributed this fog to her antipsychotic medication and her worsening dementia. I associated some of it to confusion with her move to Agrace, similar to her experience after moving to Covenant Memory Care.

As care-advocates, we are the single, consistent thread throughout our loved one's decline through dementia. Through our visits, we give our loved ones some consistency, which is something they can hang onto. Each of us is different. For me, this consistency on my part kept me focused on and tethered to Sally. For other people, the dissonance of reciprocity in the relationship may feel like a greater burden. In any event, we show up for someone who is becoming more and more absent, but we can only do so much. We can only reach the inner world of our loved ones through our love. We can't stop the dementia. The bottom line is always to trust what you witness, what you know, act on this trust, and when needed, pass on what you observe to staff members.

We were entering a new phase of Sally's care, but there were some uplifting aspects of her life at this time, too. Her room was attractive with a lovely view of an outdoor patio and a wooded area beyond it. She enjoyed being wheeled around the hallways and down the wing to her room, all the while remarking about the beauty of the artwork on the walls. Knowing that Sally liked Agrace lifted my spirits as well, and it dispelled some of the gloom surrounding her UW Hospital stay and before that, life in Covenant Memory Care. These times of reprieve and pleasure are a valuable part of the care-advocate's self-care and emotional health.

When on earlier occasions I'd visited with several residents I had known over the years who were nearing the end of their lives, I found them upbeat about life itself. What a wonderful spirit—a spirit I hoped Sally would be able to display as she, too, approached the end of her life. Their visiting relatives, usually adult children, seemed much more distraught about their parent's imminent end of life than did their parents who were at that stage. The offsprings' demeanor reminded me of the many middle-aged people I knew who had grieved so much when their parents died. This is not surprising because in addition to losing a beloved parent, they are losing a lifetime of fond memories as well.

Sally's Condition

After two months, I asked for a meeting with Sally's care team in order to get their assessment of Sally's condition. I came prepared with a series of questions for them: How successfully was she adapting to Agrace? How had her physical condition changed since her arrival? How long might she continue to live before dementia took its toll? My first two questions were answered. Sally continued to receive Seroquel. She also received Oxycodone for occasional pain and Haldol to deal with her agitation/delirium episodes that typically occurred in the mid to late afternoon. On how long she might live, there were no answers.

The nurse said that since Sally's admission, her condition, based on objective measures, had continued to decline. These measures included her increased agitation, reduced endurance, decreased ability to be redirected, diminished muscle mass, increased confusion, and the fact that she was hitting some of the staff members who were assisting her. She could not be bathed in the spa because the experience proved to be too overwhelming for her. Sally's weight remained constant at about 150 pounds.

At this point, I learned that for Sally to remain at Agrace, Medicare required that her condition continue to decline. The staff would have to assert in writing that she had less than six months to live. Otherwise, she would have to be transferred to another facility. This was not a happy prospect to face, but there was nothing I could do—the rules were the rules, and they were enforced.

At my mid-January 2014 meeting with Sally's care team, however, I was relieved to find out that Sally would be recertified. I learned there is nothing you can do to influence the recertification process, for the condition of your loved one determines their fate. If you find yourself in a similar situation, you should try to accept this as well.

Sally's Interactions

Sally soon became well known for her background as an English teacher and her love of words. This was revealed in her interactions with the staff; she often corrected their grammatical errors or played with the words they had uttered. At other times, though, I noticed Sally would often begin to say something and then stop. Because of her memory loss, she couldn't find the words needed to finish her sentence. However, rather than fretting about it, one needs to realize this is characteristic of many people with dementia.

We were lucky to be at Agrace, for the staff there was very involved with Sally's hour-by-hour care, making sure she was attended to and her monotony relieved. When I visited, a volunteer would often be in Sally's room reading to her, or a volunteer might be wheeling her through the large facility. Sally often seemed confused about where she was, however. After living at Agrace for a month or two, Sally remarked to me one day, "This is a very nice place. Next summer we should plan to spend a month here."

I VISITED SALLY REGULARLY, often to eat meals with her. The staff viewed her appetite as quite good most of the time. She slept well at night, and based on what the staff reported to me, she also slept a lot during the day. On numerous occasions when I arrived she would be sleeping or would want to do so, often falling asleep as I was leaving, if not before then.

Her mood varied widely, and overall, she seemed tired. Consequently, our conversations were limited. Despite my efforts to interact with my wife, her dementia thwarted my best efforts.

We have to accustom ourselves to the varying moods of our loved one and their various behaviors and try not to be too upset by them. Limited by their dementia, they are doing the best they can. We all have our limits—our loved ones and us as their caretaker-advocate. An awareness of our limits can generate a compassion for ourselves and also for them as we traverse this difficult path together.

Intellectual Stimulation

I tried to stimulate Sally by reading letters to her, most importantly the ones from a niece who visited occasionally and one from a woman who many years earlier had babysat our children. I doubt that Sally had any recollection of these two old friends or any appreciation for the contents of these letters, which I'd hoped would activate her long-term memories. That effort failed. I also read letters I solicited from former colleagues, hoping to trigger recollections of Sally's long teaching career. Again, no luck.

My experience reveals just how difficult it can be in trying to revive old memories. For me these experiences indicated quite clearly the steady advance of Sally's dementia. This realization of her memory loss greatly saddened me because I enjoyed reading these letters from Sally's old friends. In short, I gained more from them than Sally did. This may be true for you as well. However, it certainly doesn't hurt to hold this sweet space with our loved ones through the reading of letters and simply visiting over our shared memories, for we carry the memories of our loved ones on in us.

In the end, my assessment of Sally's memory was confirmed when our two daughters visited about five months after Sally entered Agrace; they concluded their mother no longer had any idea who they were. Sally did respond more favorably to the companion care people who visited her every day. Though at times Sally could be in a foul mood, these young women provided needed stimulation for Sally.

One particular volunteer, who had quite recently watched both her parents succumb to dementia, found ways to engage Sally. She enjoyed working with her because of Sally's still-lively mind and her wide experience. I believe these once-a-week sessions were most helpful in providing the kind of intellectual stimulation Sally needed. This, too, can be a reminder to allow others to use their experience and expertise; we don't have to carry this burden alone.

Goodnight Moments

There were some charming moments, and if you experience some of the same with your loved one, I encourage you to write them down so you don't become overwhelmed by what can be a steady stream of less-favorable news. An example of what I consider a charming moment: Sally loved to sit at the nurses' station where she could listen in on the talk and correct the mispronunciations of the staff.

Another example: One morning as I approached Sally's room, I could hear her speaking in an animated way. I assumed she was visiting with an Agrace volunteer. When I walked quietly into her room, I saw her sitting in her wheelchair facing the windows, by herself, and unaware of my presence. I had a good opportunity to observe Sally as she read aloud from a book containing stories about cats. Sally was a lifelong lover of cats, and we'd had several over the course of our married life. Although generally unsentimental about humanity, she had a pronounced warm spot for the various feline friends that had kept her company over the years.

As she flipped through the book's pages starting from the back of the book, she read aloud or tried to read the chapter titles printed in large, bold type. She read out loud: "The Guard Cat," and after a pause, she commented, "I wonder what it's guarding." Then I heard her read "The Ransom Hunters," followed by "I wonder what that's all about." Next "Seeing Eye Cat," followed by "Hmmm. That sounds strange." Then "Franklin and Bernice," followed by "I can't pronounce that name." She continued on through the rest of a book, which a volunteer had brought her from the Agrace library. She reminded me of our daughters, who as young children would often read aloud to themselves from their books, among them *Goodnight, Moon,* pretending they were reading by remembering the words we had read to them earlier.

Another charming moment occurred when Sally wanted to share what she observed through her windows. "I like to look at the trees outside. They are so beautiful. And the wind is blowing the leaves. The flowers are so pretty," she remarked to me. I stood there amazed by what she could tell me about what she saw. Her comments revealed the person she had once been. On occasions like that I wondered if Sally was really suffering from dementia. You might find yourself asking the same question about your loved one. We observe them as they observe their environment. How strange it must be inside a loved one's mind, watching as the world fades from them.

As time passed, Sally continued to change. Initially, she behaved passively during the once-a-week craft sessions. After several months, she began to take a more active role. In fact, she seemed to enjoy making things but could do so only with the active help of the several talented volunteers who staffed these sessions. She also responded well to volunteers who worked with her.

On the occasion of Sally's eighty-fifth birthday, I baked her favorite multilayered ambrosia cake, drawing upon a time-honored recipe in the *New York Times Cookbook* (1981). Ellen was visiting, and she and I lunched with Sally and cut the cake afterward. Sally devoured four pieces of the thickly frosted cake with its fruit-enhanced filling. After that, she was ready for a nap. Before she drifted off to sleep, I turned on her CD with its much-loved hymns sung by the Oxford University King's College Choir.

My memories of Sally are far richer and more extensive than I can present here. I am sure that after I die, my daughters will retain many memories of me but will never be able to remember all of them.

Visitors

Visits to your loved one by friends and even relatives are probably more important to you than to them. Though you are happy that friends still remember your loved one, your friends will have difficulty connecting with someone who is absent because of dementia. Sally had relatively few visitors, a common problem for most people suffering from dementia. Whether she recognized those friends who did visit was never clear. Several longtime friends then living at Oakwood Village told me later about their difficulties conversing with Sally, who they had long known as an excellent conversationalist. Who can blame them for not coming back, a situation made worse for them by their own difficulties in journeying to Agrace. I found that I rarely went back to visit Sally's fellow residents in Covenant Oaks.

The challenges of trying to have meaningful conversations with them was too much for me, as it would probably be for most other visitors. I know that experts say such visits are good for residents, but that may be a delusion. The underlying problem for me was the lack of personal stimulation resulting from such visits with friends, specifically trying to converse with people who are no longer the people they once were. So there must be both self-compassion and compassion for others who find such visitations a challenge. The one suffering from dementia likely doesn't notice the absence of others.

Sally and I had a dear friend, a retired geography professor. During the course of our friendship we had met with him regularly at Starbucks for Saturday morning coffee. After Sally had moved to Covenant Oaks, he visited Sally once, but soon realized she was no longer the stimulating conversationalist she once had been. Another of Sally's dearest friends, a former English as a Second Language conversational partner from Thailand, stopped by when she returned to the United States for a brief visit. Sally, however, had great difficulty relating to her even though beforehand I had invited several Thai students to come and read chapters from this woman's interesting new book to Sally.

During my frequent visits to my wife, I never knew quite what to expect. I did know that she would eagerly devour the piece of chocolate I always brought. Most of the time, she would be tired or sleeping while on other occasions, she could be quite lively and alert. She frequently displayed some of that agitation and anxiety I had first seen when she was at Covenant Memory Care. On some occasions she would ignore me completely. At other times she could be all sweetness, looking at me smilingly and telling me how much she loved me. She would often smile at my humorous remarks, whether she recognized me or not. Ah, the old Sally was back with me—if only momentarily.

On some visits, Sally would latch onto a question and keep repeating it. One was "What next, what next?" Another was "Let's go, let's go, why don't we go?" While the meaning of the second statement seemed apparent—that Sally wanted to be more active and go back home—the meaning of the first was not at all clear. These outbursts of hers were distressing, but at least she wasn't asking me to help her die. Maybe she was expressing her impatience and wanting to be active and moving about rather than confined to her wheelchair or bed. Maybe those were times she thought we were in a resort and wanted to know what was next on the social schedule. Not being able to fully grasp what our loved ones mean becomes a constant in a sea of changes. I did my best to guess and respond, though less successfully than I'd hoped to do.

Again, compassion is the best antidote here for all. As a caregiver, you will face similar situations that can easily leave you confused and disappointed, but don't give up on yourself or your loved one. Do what you can to stay active in a conversation, but let the expectations go, as best you can. Cherish the small moments of connection, humor, and love. Even as they lose their memory they can feel your love, your presence, and your help.

Hospice is For the Dying

Agrace Hospice Care was established to accommodate the dying and to assist the families of the dying. But there are also people with dementia and other long-term conditions that need the care that only hospice can provide. As we all know, predicting how long someone with dementia will live is virtually impossible. After completing her second three months at Agrace, Sally's care team concluded that her condition had stabilized. This meant that she could remain at Agrace until her next evaluation in another sixty days. I was told then that unless something serious happened, it seemed unlikely she would be able to remain at Agrace beyond that time, simply because her condition was not worsening. I was greatly disappointed to hear this because Agrace was so well equipped and had, up until then, worked out quite well.

Sally continued to receive Seroquel. At times she would become agitated, but not to the same degree as previously at Covenant Memory Care. On these occasions, she would be given Lorazepam, which is a fast-acting and effective calming agent. Toward the end of her sixth month at Agrace, the staff talked about slowly reducing her Seroquel dosage because its effectiveness diminishes over time. Its policy called for giving residents only those medications deemed absolutely essential for their well-being. To my surprise, Agrace took no action to stop giving her Seroquel. I think the staff realized that the timing for such a change would not be ideal if Sally had to be moved elsewhere.

Moving Again

The prospect of having to move Sally once more was discouraging. She had already been moved nine times since leaving our old home and seven times since she'd left Covenant Memory Care. No wonder she often seemed confused about where she was and perhaps even who she still was. In these situations, it is important for you to be at hand to provide a personal connection and link to your loved one's fading past.

Though I had been given a month to relocate Sally, I asked to put off the search until early September so I could spend a week in Door County with our daughter, Ellen, and her family. Upon my return, I began the search. Over the next two weeks, I visited and considered eight excellent assisted-living communities in the Madison area where I live. The search took a toll because in a short visit one cannot learn very much about what life will be like in another institution. This uncertainty was made even more trying after Sally's wonderful stay at Agrace. Could any other end-of-life community be better for her?

Three considerations dominated my search: what kind of care each facility provided, my estimation of the quality of care each provided, and the availability of space. These facilities offered a wide variety of possibilities, from general assisted living to support for memory impairment to skilled nursing care. I toured most of these facilities and had in-depth discussions with the staff at several of them.

Making a selection was complicated by the fact that Sally needed something more than the services they offered at Oakwood's Covenant Memory Care but something less than Oakwood's Hebron skilled nursing care. By the end of an intensive week of searching, I found what seemed like the ideal end-of-life care community that just happened to be located only a few blocks away from where I lived in Oakwood Village.

When the time came to move Sally, many Agrace staff members and volunteers crowded into her room to say farewell. Sally beamed from the attention. Though greatly touched by this outpouring of affection for my wife, I wished there had been some way for her to remain at Agrace. Sally wished them all well as the ambulance staff wheeled her off for a trip to her next destination.

Part III

A Final Move

"Autumn Song" by Dante Gabriel Rossetti

Know'st thou not at the fall of the leaf
How the heart feels a languid grief
Laid on it for a covering,
And how sleep seems a goodly thing
In Autumn at the fall of the leaf?

And how the swift beat of the brain
Falters because it is in vain,
In Autumn at the fall of the leaf
Knowest thou not? And how the chief
Of joys seems—not to suffer pain?

Know'st thou not at the fall of the leaf
How the soul feels like a dried sheaf
Bound up at length for harvesting,
And how death seems a comely thing
In Autumn at the fall of the leaf?

Chapter 8

ADAPTING AND RENEWED AGITATION IN MEMORY CARE

THE ASSISTED-LIVING facility that most impressed me turned out to be a for-profit senior living community located on Madison's west side. BrightStar Senior Living's newly constructed residential care unit, completed only six months earlier in March 2014, could accommodate Sally immediately.

As she settled in to BrightStar, I realized how fortunate I was to be able to select among Madison's numerous high-quality, memory-care communities, particularly one with an environment similar to that of Agrace Hospice Care. By this I mean a community characterized by a quiet, homelike atmosphere, accommodating a limited number of residents who suffered from dementia, and employing a fully engaged, experienced professional staff—in particular an active director and a talented wellness nurse.

I fully realize that not every family can have access to this kind of care. Not only were many choices open to me, but I could afford to pay the associated costs. Because both Sally and I had worked at well-paying jobs and we'd lived modestly over the years, we were not financially constrained. Many families, however, cannot afford this level of care and must tend to their loved ones at home, sometimes having to give up their paying jobs to serve as full-time caregivers. Nor can they afford home-comfort care; the cost is simply beyond their capacity to pay.

Sally's placement at BrightStar came as near to ideal as any loved one could hope for, offering—in my estimation—the best and highest quality of care appropriate for a person with Sally's advanced stage of dementia. With enhanced universal health care and improved elder care, perhaps this ideal template will become more prevalent across the United States. This is not the case now, and achieving this relies on us as advocates to help transform and update the health care system.

Please use this chapter as a template and perhaps an inspiration so that together we may effect positive change in this sector of the U.S. health care system. We are an aging population and can influence the direction of policy and services when and where we put our hearts and minds to it.

BrightStar as the Ideal

Because BrightStar was my first extended exposure to an assisted-living/memory-care/end-of-life environment, I want to describe its atmosphere and what we all want for our loved ones who suffer from dementia. I highlight those characteristics of BrightStar that proved to be decisive in my decision to locate Sally there. I suggest you use my experience with BrightStar as a checklist for what to look for when you seek not only memory care for your loved one but also public policy programs that you may want to advocate for.

Getting Acquainted

What made BrightStar so attractive as a home for Sally was its small size and its emphasis on end-of-life care. In addition, the building's two-story design and layout did not feature the interminably long hallways so frequently found in single-story buildings. Equally important, it separated the dozen or so assisted-living residents on the first floor from the dozen or so residents with dementia living on the second floor. The small number of second-floor residents made for a more peaceful atmosphere overall.

This two-story arrangement, with controlled access to both the building and to the second floor, provided ample security for everyone. It also permitted some degree of specialization among the resident assistant staff members, and it made it easier for them to know the residents and the kind of care they needed. These are important considerations to keep in mind when selecting end-of-life care for your loved one, particularly if they suffer from serious anxiety and agitation as Sally did.

Considerable thought had gone into the design of the resident rooms and the commons areas. Each room included an ample-sized bathroom with a walk-in shower, a closet, and in the entryway, a sink, small stove, and small fridge. Families were expected to provide the furniture, such as a bed, a table and lamp, chairs, and whatever other decorations might help the resident feel at home.

Similar thought had gone into the design of the commons areas. Each floor had an attractive living room area that featured a fireplace, a love seat, several comfortable, overstuffed chairs, and several other chairs as well as an end table or two with a lamp on top. An adjacent activity area, furnished with a half-dozen tables and chairs, doubled as a dining room, with a small but fully equipped kitchen and a serving area off to one side. Two smaller areas were nearby—one a library alcove and the other a family meeting room. Except for the latter, these spaces were fully visible to the resident assistants in the commons area. Nearby was a large separate "wellness" room where new resident assistants were trained and where meetings with family members could be held. While the first-floor activity area was larger than its equivalent on the second floor, the second floor had a spacious, uncovered sun porch available for use in the spring, summer, and fall. It featured large glass panels that blocked out the wind and gave residents maximum visibility of pedestrian and street traffic below.

The building was designed to meet the needs of assisted living residents who wanted larger rooms and a more homelike commons area. It served as a prototype for a similar building recently completed in nearby Waunakee, Wisconsin, and will be used as a model for other residential care facilities around the country. While more and more facilities are being constructed for the ever-growing population of people with memory loss, they must be designed to appeal to families. For-profit institutions such as BrightStar will continue to increase, and pressure will mount for public subsidization of additional memory-care facilities.

Major efforts are now being made to facilitate more home health care, both to accommodate the wishes of many elders who wish to remain in their homes and to help hold down the private and public costs of end-of-life care. For this effort to succeed people are going to need help in making their homes both safe and suitable to accommodate them as they age. They will also need periodic attention from medical personnel to ensure that they remain as healthy as they can be, are adequately fed, and their personal needs are adequately cared for. Here in Madison, many elderly people already receive regular home care from hospice personnel and in some cases from private home-care personnel.

Readers should make good use of community services for the elderly, which are provided by public agencies for the aged, the Alzheimer's Association, and local volunteer agencies. These organizations can direct family members to other organizations that can provide home health care, to groups that can provide support to family caregivers, and to advocacy groups that promote legislation to help people with limited financial resources.

(The Ideal) Professional Staff

Having had vast experience in assisted-living and memory-care facilities, BrightStar's staff demonstrated the knowledge and commitment needed to provide top-notch quality care to its residents. This is something we should expect at such facilities. Ideally, staff and healthcare providers will be intimately involved in the care of each resident, and consequently, their knowledge of every resident will be both wide and deep, as was the case at BrightStar. Staff members were saddened as they witnessed the physical and mental decline and eventual death of the residents in turn; in this they suffered along with the family caregivers.

The life-enrichment coordinator and her activity assistant play vital roles in keeping residents occupied constructively day after day. Typically, these people have college degrees, most frequently in the field of social work. Some have additional certifications in the care of people with dementia.

Resident assistants have a large role to play. We will discuss them next.

Resident Assistant Staff

In an ideal facility such as BrightStar, a large staff of trained resident assistants is maintained to staff both floors and all three eight-hour shifts. Two resident assistants are constantly present during the day to assist second-floor residents who suffer from dementia. This means helping them get up and get dressed in the morning and assisting in their toileting and personal care, making certain their teeth are brushed, selecting their clothing for the day, and helping feed those who need such help. This care also involves helping the residents into and out of their beds and wheelchairs when they want to rest and helping them get ready for bed at night.

Resident assistants must be on constant alert to assist the residents in any and all ways needed. If a resident is tired and wants to take a nap, the assistants help them. When a resident is confused, resident assistants help them straighten out their confusion by redirecting their attention. If they are bothering other residents (which often happens during daily scheduled activities), resident assistants come forward to redirect the offending resident, usually by moving that person away from others.

Resident assistants must be ready to step forward and redirect residents because their brains no longer function as they once did. That said, the goal is to help residents make their own decisions about what to do next. Throughout the day, resident assistants must demonstrate the kind of patience most of us would find difficult to maintain.

Almost all of the resident assistants at BrightStar were young women, many of whom were working to complete their certified nursing assistant (CNA) certification. Others had already been CNA certified. Still others were studying to become registered nurses. The key to compiling an effective staff of resident assistants is careful selection in the hiring process, comprehensive training, and periodic retraining that reinforces their initial training and broadens their expertise.

What all family members and care-advocates should look for are resident assistants who are skillful in carrying out their duties, compassionate in working with residents, and mindful of the cooperative nature of their profession. They constitute the frontline givers in every memory-care institution. Their effectiveness depends heavily on their supervision, their training, and their constant retraining. Loved ones should certainly inquire about the background and training of these key people.

Daily Schedule

The daily schedule at BrightStar begins sometime before 7:00 a.m., when residents are aided in getting up, dressed, and moved to the commons area to be ready for morning breakfast served at 8:00. Medications scheduled to be taken in the morning are dispensed after residents finish eating. Residents may be taken to their rooms after breakfast to be toileted unless they choose to remain in the commons living room and listen to music or watch television. At 9:30 a.m., the daily life-enrichment programs begin and continue until 11:30 a.m. Lunch is served at noon, along with any needed medications. After lunch, residents rest or watch TV until the afternoon activities begin at 1:30 or 2:00 p.m. These activities continue until about 4:00 p.m. This allows an hour for residents to rest, listen to music, or watch TV before supper, which is served about 5:00 p.m. along with the administration of evening medications. After supper, residents usually want to go to their rooms and get ready for bed. Most residents are in bed by 7:00 p.m. and are soon asleep.

A wellness nurse checks the status of all of the residents every morning, which includes paying particular attention to those residents who may have experienced some incident the previous night. A standard protocol exists for reporting these incidents. Throughout the day, the wellness nurse is available to deal with the special needs of particular residents. She also trains newly hired resident assistants and conducts ongoing training programs for the resident assistants who are on staff. Every three months the Individualized Service Plan for each resident is updated and revised as necessary.

The schedule of daily activities, planned and led by the life-enrichment coordinator, offers wide-ranging physical and mental stimulation to residents. These activities occur in the dining room that doubles as an activity room. Every weekend a daily schedule of the following week's events is published, and every day there are five to six scheduled activities. The morning events typically include a half-hour session of low-intensity exercise, reading from the local newspaper, a session to stimulate the mind by engaging residents in solving puzzles, mind-teasing activities, listening to stories, and so on. The afternoon events put greater emphasis on music and the arts and may include an illustrated lecture presentation, an hour-long musical presentation featuring piano, accordion, or wind instruments by an outsider, or some other group activity.

Family members should try to visit during the day so they can observe what is being done to enrich the lives of the residents. They should also take the opportunity to recommend to the facility's director and to its nurse other activities they believe might help their loved one and perhaps most of the other residents as well. Showing an interest in the community's operations and suggesting possible improvements, even if they cannot be instituted, is a way of demonstrating to the staff how much you value their good work and are thinking about how it may be enhanced.

Other Residents

Just as anywhere else, residents differ physically, cognitively, and emotionally. No matter how dissimilar residents might have been before the onset of their dementia, the differences among them gradually widen as the dementia takes hold. These differences are often revealed by their conscious and unconscious behaviors. At BrightStar, one resident had served in the famous 101st Airborne Division in World War II and was very proud of it. One day I overhead him talking about the war and the roles played by the different branches of the U. S. military. Another very sweet woman could not say much more than describe where she'd grown up and gone to college, but she delighted in displaying the colorful bracelets and necklaces that the staff adorned her with every day. Other residents were rarely sighted or said little.

It quickly becomes apparent that residents come from similar backgrounds—mostly white, upper-income families that can afford to pay the substantial monthly fees, fees that are not covered by Medicare. It is rare to find members of minority groups living in communities such as BrightStar because the cost is so high.

In addition to this, learning more about the other residents is a challenge due to privacy laws. Staff members understand they cannot divulge any details about the earlier lives of the residents. As a result, residents become the forgotten because their stories and memories disappear. Their memories are not reinforced because these folks can no longer be reminded of the people they once were. How sad this is—because we are our stories and experiences.

Knowing something about the lives of the residents would have made it easier for visitors like me to engage at least some of them. Only when family members visited did I have a chance to find out more about the interesting lives so many residents had lived before their dementia took hold.

This emphasis on privacy, though well-intended, cuts residents off from their histories and makes connecting with them more difficult for everyone. Family members who spend considerable time with the residents are likely to pick up scraps of information that may enable them to interact with other residents in addition to their loved ones.

In Sally's case, I tried to help by encouraging the staff to open a three-ring binder in her room that contained extensive information about her upbringing in Detroit, her education in the field of English, our two daughters, her teaching career, and the English as a Second Language mentoring and teaching work she'd done.

When new residents are admitted to a care facility, their families should be encouraged to provide information that will help staff and others realize they are dealing with real people rather than the shells of formerly interesting and vibrant people. Everyone likes to be asked about their lives; doing so is much easier if you have a snippet of information, enough to help you formulate a question to the resident. Even if they cannot respond, you will have helped them.

Then there is the inevitable arrival of new residents who replace those who have recently passed away. Resident turnover is quite rapid. Among the roughly dozen residents on the dementia floor at the time of Sally's death, only two dementia-afflicted residents had lived at BrightStar longer than Sally had. Sally resided there for only eighteen months. Meanwhile, still other residents had come and gone while Sally continued on. The constant reminder that death is a reality is something family members must adjust to, and in so doing, they may find it easier to accept the death of their loved one when the time arrives.

Outreach to Families

The BrightStar staff offers a late afternoon Resident and Family Council program once a month. These meetings are open to residents as well as family care-advocates; all are encouraged to attend. The purpose of these meetings is to help family members gain a better understanding of how BrightStar operates. This is certainly something every facility could provide.

During the first few months of Sally's residence at BrightStar, I heard informative presentations by the executive director, the health and wellness nurse, the life enrichment coordinator, the pharmacist who supplied BrightStar with its medications, and the chef. The quality of these presentations always impressed me, and I was constantly surprised at how few family members attended them, perhaps because the meeting time, typically 4:00 to 5:00 p.m., interfered with their jobs.

Once a month, there is a community dinner to which family caregivers are invited. The menus vary and are often suggested by residents and resident assistants. These dinners offer a good opportunity to meet other caregivers and observe their relationships with their loved one.

At BrightStar, much is made of traditional holidays, among them Christmas, Thanksgiving, Easter, Memorial Day, the Fourth of July, Labor Day, and Thanksgiving. (Residents' birthdays are also honored with a birthday cake.) To help celebrate these special days, family members as well as the children of the resident assistants are often invited to participate in the commemorative event of the particular day. Not only do the children enjoy themselves but the residents get a chance to meet and interact with these kids who they would not otherwise see. Staff members get an opportunity to involve their young children in the day's activities. These are always charming events that are enjoyed by everyone.

Related Services

The BrightStar staff believed that keeping Sally busy and engaged would reduce her agitation and anxiety. To address this, they were able to provide additional services. These included making nurses and other caregivers available to help those individuals who needed additional care, often during their final days. To provide additional personal interaction, I employed

BrightStar Home Care companion caregivers to spend three hours every afternoon with my wife. These women met and talked with Sally, trying to engage her in conversations about her life and interests. Family members need to know about the availability of this extra care, though the personal expense may dissuade them from using it.

How the World Works

No institution operates as effectively and perfectly as we would like it to. I realize that staff members, facilities, and families vary widely in their background, training, and performance. And while improvements may be suggested, they are often difficult to implement and achieve. This is the way the world works. But let's not forget that every time we ask for what we want, speak up when we see problems, or advocate for better care, we are making a difference.

In addition to the limitations listed above, the behavior of other family caregivers often differs, particularly those whose loved one may have been in another facility and was moved to BrightStar because of a dissatisfaction with the previous facility. These differing perspectives can come to light only when family caregivers assemble together. When they do, they voice not only their particular concerns about the care of their loved ones but also broader concerns that affect the lives of the whole group of residents. Resolving these concerns is an important task in the never-ending effort to improve the quality of care for those who suffer from dementia.

Relations with BrightStar Staff

Through my frequent visits to BrightStar and my obvious love and concern for Sally, I developed close relations with the BrightStar staff. This is one of the most important things family members can do because so often there is little one can directly do to help their loved one. Unless you are very obnoxious, caregivers welcome your interest and attention. They like to be called upon to display their knowledge and skills and to be treated with respect.

I felt that my attention to the BrightStar staff and particularly the wellness nurse paid off handsomely—I was able to learn so much because of the serious questions I posed. Establishing this trust is not that difficult; family members need to show their respect for the staff and what they know. At the same time they need to ask about any worrisome aspects of the care being given to their loved one.

I suspect I had more interactions with staff members than most family caregivers-advocates do. But this is an essential part of our advocacy: to develop and value these relationships as best we can. While I continued to read about dementia in its various forms, the staff helped me as I kept trying to learn more about what makes dementia residents act as they do. At the same time, I realized that attempting to explain Sally's behavior was like trying to peer into an intricate piece of machinery whose inner workings were not visible from the outside.

State Inspection Results

Added support for my decision to select BrightStar came from the reports of state inspections conducted by the Wisconsin Department of Health Services. Its staff makes surprise visits to assisted-living care facilities to check on their compliance with the state regulations that govern the operations of these organizations. I happened to be visiting Sally at BrightStar on the days of two such inspections, the most recent only two months before she died. The inspector questioned me carefully about any concerns I had about the staff and the quality of care Sally was receiving. My comments were highly favorable for the reasons already discussed.

In March 2016, the executive director sent a letter to residents and families reporting on the January inspection. She indicated that this unannounced survey had resulted in BrightStar's fourth citation-free survey in two years. She detailed the coverage of the inspection and added that these inspections encourage self-examination, which produces ideas for improving BrightStar's operation.

Remembrances

Approximately once a year, an afternoon remembrance ceremony is organized to honor BrightStar residents who passed away the previous year. Family members of deceased residents are invited to attend. Each former resident is named, and something is said about the uniqueness of their lives and their lives at BrightStar. Though the comments were typically brief, I gained insight into the life of a colleague who was a twenty-year-long member of a book group I belonged to. In several cases, I learned about the interesting, early careers of different women before they'd married and started raising their children.

Sally's Arrival

When Sally had arrived at BrightStar in late September 2014, nobody knew or could know how long she might remain there. More important, I saw none of the agitation and anxiety that had led to her removal from Covenant Oaks. I hoped that the quiet atmosphere at Agrace Hospice and the continued administration of Seroquel would smooth her transition.

Sally's adjustment to BrightStar was eased by the considerable similarities in the physical structures of BrightStar and Agrace. Both were quite new and had fresh looks about them, with lots of light coming in the windows and a variety of striking wall hangings. I hoped that with the arrival of Sally's furniture and framed pictures from Agrace Hospice, her transition would be eased. Under ideal circumstances, she might not even realize she had been moved. That proved to be the case.

Sally adjusted to BrightStar faster and much better than I expected. The Agrace Hospice staff warned me that change is always difficult for people suffering from dementia. I thought this change would be especially hard for Sally because she'd received so much attention from the Agrace staff. Nonetheless, she settled in to BrightStar without much agitation or anxiety. While I would not describe Sally as happy, neither would I say she was unhappy. I hoped that with time she would reach a stage that could best be described as "contented."

My initial assessment of Sally's move to BrightStar was confirmed by the wellness nurse who described her initial encounter with Sally as follows: "I spent some time with Sally yesterday. Some happy, some sad. She was certain for most of the day that her mother was dying and she needed to get to her. There were many tears and no easy redirection so I just held her hand and let her cry. Having supper changed her direction on its own. We had a good discussion about grammar, music, and how she feels I should quit talking to one of the other residents because he is 'never going to understand fully what you are saying anyway.' She quickly formed an attachment to Lois, one of our activity's assistants. 'Hello Lois.' 'Where's Lois?' 'You're not Lois.' 'Why isn't Lois serving me ice cream?' It was sweet. All in all, I believe we have had an easy transition and she has slid into life in the memory-care household with ease."

I quickly became acquainted with other family caregivers when they visited or dined with their loved ones. They all spoke of the difficulties they struggled with in terms of how to best care for their loved one. They all seemed to realize that they faced a host of unknowns, wondering what accounted for dementia, how rapidly it would progress, and how long their loved one would remain alive. They also mentioned the unpredictable moods and unexpected behavioral changes they so frequently witnessed. I believe we all came to realize we were in this together and would simply have to stick it out until our loved ones passed away.

Most distressing was Sally's inability to recognize our daughters when they visited, and it was always heartbreaking to hear Sally ask me, "And who are you?" At other times, I was not sure she knew who *I* was until I began speaking.

About Falling

I soon learned that Sally experienced skin burns when she got out of bed at night to move down the hallway to the commons area. She did this by sliding out of bed onto the rubber mats beside the bed and then propelling herself out of her room and down the hallway. She extended her feet out in front of her and then used her legs to pull her body along the floor. Often she would be discovered halfway down the hall. In the process, she developed and worsened the skin abrasions already evident on her back and buttocks.

"Take Me Home"

When I visited Sally, a recurrent theme was her plea to take her "home." Paradoxically, she often talked about what a wonderful place BrightStar was, how nice her room was, how good the food was, and so on. But on other occasions she cried out for help. "Help me, help me!" This seemed to indicate that her agitation and anxiety were not thoroughly subdued by her regularly scheduled Seroquel medication. I took some small comfort in the fact that she wasn't asking me to help her die, as she typically did in outbursts like this, although she might still have wanted me to do so.

When I explained that I couldn't take her home because the house had been sold, she showed frustration but found herself unable to respond. Her difficulty in communicating was often illustrated by her inability to complete a sentence once she'd started it. For example, at times she would add that "something is wrong with my brain" but she couldn't go beyond that. I found it so sad that this talented woman, a lover of words, could no longer express her thoughts as she'd once been able to do.

To summarize, Sally's behavior in her first few months at BrightStar became increasingly varied and unpredictable. Sometime in January 2015, the staff recommended that her regular dosage of Seroquel be phased out because its effectiveness seemed to be diminishing. How much her agitation and anxiety would increase was anybody's guess. As it turned out, Sally's agitation and anxiety did increase as BrightStar began to reduce her regular doses of Seroquel at two-week intervals.

Chapter 9

MILESTONES THAT MARKED OUR LIVES

SUMMER 2015 PASSED quickly, and fall came and went. Soon we were in December. During the summer months, Sally's condition improved, partly as a result of the medication change and partly because of the presence of daily companion care, or so I assumed. In August, Agrace nursing care was added to deal with Sally's frequent skin tears and more frequent falls. By October, Sally's agitation returned and steadily worsened through November and early December. This development required giving her ever-stronger and more-frequent dosages of an antipsychotic, Haldol. Sally was no longer encouraged to engage in group activities because they only worsened her condition.

How discouraging. I reluctantly concluded Sally was in the midst of a long, slow period of decline, and I realized I would have to accept this inevitability. Though her condition would continue to vary in unpredictable ways, eventually her dementia would undermine her health and bring about her death.

The BrightStar nurse reported a new development to me: Sally always seemed to be hungry between meals. It was as if she had developed a new between-meal fixation on food and drink. The staff was always happy to give her juice or ice cream. She was also allowed to go into the kitchen and take whatever she could find in the fridge. But when she was discovered drinking juice directly out of the container, the staff felt they had to do something, and that was to install a lock on the fridge door to prevent her nocturnal sipping from the juice container.

The woman who ran the BrightStar companion-care programs sent a kind note telling me about a charming, recent encounter with Sally that had occurred when she was in the building giving a tour to another senior living professional. This is what she wrote: "When I entered the upstairs great room, Sally reached out her hand to me and asked who we were. I took her hand and told her my name and that I knew her husband, Lee. She asked if I spelled my name with an I or a Y. I said, with a Y and asked her how she spelled Sally. She said it was with a Y, too, and said she also knew a Lee, then spelled H-a-n-s-e-n. She held my hand tightly and said, 'I'm so glad I found you. Let's hold onto each other so we don't lose one another.' One of the caregivers had to come and get Sally so I could continue with the tour. Thought you'd like to know what a gracious greeting she gave us."

Our Sixtieth Wedding Anniversary

I soon began wondering whether Sally would live long enough for us to celebrate our sixtieth wedding anniversary together in late December. I would be away visiting our two daughters at Christmas but planned to return immediately after that. As it worked out, we were able to celebrate our wedding anniversary, marking sixty years of living and working together, raising and educating our daughters, and loving each other. We had many fond memories, and they would all come together in a gala anniversary celebration.

Sally and I celebrated our sixtieth wedding anniversary on December 31, 2015. The celebration occurred at BrightStar Senior Living and was very different from our fiftieth anniversary, which we had celebrated with our family in Johannesburg, South Africa, ten years earlier. At that time our daughter, Ellen, and her husband, Harvey, lived there, along with one of their daughters. Our daughter, Martha, attended, as did all four grandchildren who flew in from England, Portland, and Peoria. We had a glorious celebration in the midst of a world of absolute poverty.

I arranged that the entire BrightStar staff be invited to attend, including the resident assistants as well as the owners of BrightStar and the families of the residents, particularly those on the second floor where Sally lived. I also asked that all BrightStar Home Care staff who provided companion care for Sally be invited, including its supervisor-director. Finally, I invited the nurse and social worker from Agrace Hospice who visited Sally once a week. I also invited three Oakwood Village staff members who were involved in Sally's care when she had resided in its Covenant Memory Care unit and the two people most involved in her care when she had resided in Agrace Hospice. As I explained to the director of BrightStar Senior Living in making the arrangements, I wanted the celebration to recognize everyone who had been involved in Sally's care over the past two and a half years. These people, who knew Sally so well, deserved to be thanked for the excellent care she had received from them.

I baked an ambrosia cake, one of Sally's favorites, for the occasion, and BrightStar baked another special cake of its own. It also provided sparkling cider for a toast. Unable to find "Happy Sixtieth Anniversary" greeting cards, even at Hallmark, and no sixtieth anniversary balloons, I improvised with a "Happy Anniversary" balloon and two others—one shaped like a 6 and the other like a 0.

I assembled a group of photos mounted on a trifold white board so people attending could learn more about the lives we had led up to that point. I included a couple of great photos from our 2005 celebration. The white board also featured a copy of my essay, "An Innocent—Or Not So Innocent—First Date?" that described how Sally and I met and fell in love.

In one of my closets, I located the lovely black outfit Sally had worn on our fiftieth anniversary, and I brought it to BrightStar. I wanted Sally to look her very best. So that we would both appear in the same garb we wore at our fiftieth, I put on my seldom-used tuxedo. At about 2:00 p.m. on that bright, clear winter afternoon, staff members began bringing residents into the dining/activity room on the second floor. Some were in wheelchairs, others were aided by their walkers, and a few were still able to maneuver on their own. Meanwhile, family members and staff members began gathering.

When Sally was wheeled in, she looked stunning in her 2005 outfit. At the same time, she seemed rather tired and was not very talkative. She kept saying softly, "Help me, help me! I want to die, please help me! Please!" She leaned forward in her wheelchair as if in distress. I tried to reassure her and so did the resident assistant with her. It was agony to see my wife in so much distress, and again, I couldn't help but wish that the appropriate legislation was in place to allow for her wish to be granted. Every time I heard her plead with me in this way, my heart broke, and I contemplated the irony yet again that as a young woman, Sally had advocated for the right to die for others in similar situations. Now she was begging for this right for herself. How inhumane it was that she had to continue to suffer so much.

At this time, the Life Enrichment Director and her assistant, aided by several resident assistants, began serving pieces of cake and distributing plastic glasses of sparkling cider. To redirect Sally's attention, I asked her if she would like a piece of cake. She immediately said yes. She wasted no time digging into the large piece of cake I cut for her. I had decorated her favourite ambrosia cake with a circle of blueberries around the top, surrounding the number 60, which was constructed in the middle with fresh raspberries. I must say that it looked scrumptious!

After eating every crumb of that first piece of cake, Sally asked for more. This time it was a piece of the chocolate/raspberry cake made by BrightStar's chef. Sally dug into the piece and soon finished it. I asked if she wanted more. She said "No, I've had enough." But in another minute or two, she began reaching for my plate and the plate of the woman next to her, trying to grab the cake from our plates. As so it went. By the end of the afternoon, Sally had probably consumed a half-dozen good-sized pieces of cake. Early on I had asked an assistant to place a large bib across her front to prevent food from dropping down onto her outfit. Several times her hands had to be washed because she ate so much of the cake with her fingers.

Later I wondered whether Sally suffered any ill-effects from gorging herself on cake. The BrightStar nurse responded, "Most people would be sick to their stomachs. I can tell you that I saw Sally all the way through to 7:00 p.m., and she looked exactly like she always does. What I know is that her eating had no effect on her."

At this point, the Life Enrichment Director asked for everyone's attention. She proposed a toast to us for our marvelous, sixty years of marriage. I responded briefly, expressing our thanks for the excellent care provided by both BrightStar Senior Living and BrightStar Home Care as well as everyone else who had provided such good care for Sally over the past almost two and a half years. Exactly what I said about the factors that had contributed to our long and successful marriage I don't recall. But it included a similarity in our intellectual interests, tolerance for our differences, patience with each other, a good sense of humor, and that ever-present factor—good luck.

I added that the chance of people like Sally and me reaching our sixtieth wedding anniversary were extremely low. By my rough estimate only about 1 percent—or about 15,000 of the 1.5 million marriages occurring in 1955—had survived to celebrate a sixtieth wedding anniversary. That is what made this day so special.

The last part of the program called for the Life Enrichment Director to read the short statements from our four grandchildren about their love and respect for their grandmother. None of them had been able to attend our wedding anniversary celebration, so their words would stand in for their actual presence. The exclamations from the assembled group indicated how impressed they were with what they heard about Sally from each of the grandkids; I had limited each of them to three-hundred-word statements!

With that, the wedding anniversary celebration ended. Some people resumed eating their ambrosia cake, most likely their second helpings. The cake was completely demolished. The several remaining pieces of the much bigger chocolate/raspberry cake were put aside to be consumed by the resident assistants working on the night shift.

Meanwhile, photos were taken, and staff mingled among the residents and family members. Many people thanked me for hosting this event. The kindest words came from the BrightStar nurse who knew and worked most closely with Sally. She commended me for being such a good husband as well as a helpful and considerate caregiver. She added, whispering quietly, that I served as a role model for the young unmarried women who worked at BrightStar as resident assistants. She added that several had expressed the hope that they might find a husband "like Mr. Hansen"—someone kind and thoughtful in his dealings with his wife and everyone at BrightStar. What a wonderful compliment! It touched me deeply.

What did I make of the celebration? I viewed it as a grand success, even though Sally could not be fully present for the occasion. When I asked her just before leaving whether she had enjoyed it, she answered graciously, "Oh, yes, I did." But whether she comprehended what had happened in the previous couple of hours is anyone's guess. Although she did murmur "yes" or "good" after Maria finished reading each statement from the grandchildren, saying for example "Yes, that's from Zachary," I'm not sure she grasped what they actually said. Whether or not Sally remembered anything about the celebration the next day was highly unlikely.

Still, the event proved to be a great success in that everyone seemed to recognize they were honoring a unique couple and a particularly interesting resident, namely Sally Porch Hansen. Yet how sad it was that after we'd experienced such a wonderful and rewarding life together, filled with mutual respect and abundant love and affection for each other, we passed this milestone with Sally unable to fully appreciate it.

Sally's Eighty-Seventh Birthday

We had one more milestone looming ahead, toward the end of January, namely Sally's eighty-seventh birthday. This called for another celebration, albeit not quite as extravagant as our wedding anniversary had been.

Before her birthday arrived, two other developments should be noted. First, BrightStar's early January review of Sally's Individual Service Plan indicated that she continued to have considerable physical strength but was failing in other ways. Though the staff tried to be upbeat, it was clear to me that Sally was in a state of serious decline. I did not press for their elaboration, realizing that Sally would soon die.

The following week, the Agrace nurses arranged for the Agrace psychiatrist to do an assessment of my wife. Throughout their meeting, Sally kept saying "The Rockies, the Rockies." The psychiatrist asked me what she might be talking about. I had no idea; we had not been to the Rockies for more than two decades. Though some minor changes were made in her medications, again, I think it was clear that Sally would soon pass away.

On Sally's birthday, January 23, Ellen drove up from Glen Ellyn, Illinois, to help celebrate. When we arrived, Sally did not recognize Ellen nor did she appreciate the significance of the occasion. I had asked that a birthday cake be baked for the event to be shared with the residents and staff.

We began by singing "Happy Birthday." Then Sally, without great effort, blew out the dozen or so candles on the cake. With that the resident assistants began cutting the cake and serving pieces to the residents. What I most remember is that Sally consumed two good-sized pieces of chocolate cake covered with a thick white frosting. After she finished off the first piece, Ellen asked her whether she was full. She said "yes." But when another piece of cake was put in front of her, she quickly gobbled it down.

Everyone attending wished Sally well.

Part IV

The Ending

"The Choir Invisible" by George Eliot

O May I join the choir invisible
Of those immortal dead who live again
In minds made better by their presence: live
In pulses stirr'd to generosity,
In deeds of daring rectitude, in scorn
For miserable aims that end with self,
In thoughts sublime that pierce the night like stars,
And with their mild persistence urge man's search
To vaster issues.
So to live is heaven:
To make undying music in the world,
Breathing as beauteous order that controls
With growing sway the growing life of man.
So we inherit that sweet purity
For which we struggled, fail'd, and agoniz'd
With widening retrospect that bred despair.
Rebellious flesh that would not be subdued,
A vicious parent shaming still its child,
Poor anxious penitence, is quick dissolv'd;

Its discords, quench'd by meeting harmonies,
Die in the large and charitable air.
And all our rarer, better, truer self,
That sobb'd religiously in yearning song,
That watch'd to ease the burthen of the world,
Laboriously tracing what must be,
And what may yet be better,—saw within
A worthier image for the sanctuary,
And shap'd it forth before the multitude,
Divinely human, raising worship so
To higher reverence more mix'd with love,—
That better self shall live till human Time
Shall fold its eyelids, and the human sky
Be gather'd like a scroll within the tomb Unread forever.
This is life to come,
Which martyr'd men have made more glorious
For us who strive to follow. May I reach
That purest heaven, be to other souls
The cup of strength in some great agony,
Enkindle generous ardor, feed pure love,
Beget the smiles that have no cruelty,
Be the sweet presence of a good diffus'd,
And in diffusion ever more intense!
So shall I join the choir invisible
Whose music is the gladness of the world.

Chapter 10

SALLY SLIPS AWAY

WITH EACH SETBACK of Sally's, a part of me died. Bit by bit, the wonderful life we shared slipped and broke away like the calving of the glaciers she and I had witnessed on a trip to Alaska a few years earlier. Sally slipped into the darkness of dementia while I slipped into the world of a husband grieving through the end of more than sixty years of a loving, stimulating marriage. I constantly missed the presence of the Sally I knew, who had made life so meaningful and challenging for me.

When my thoughts took me to places where I tried to pick up pieces of our wonderful life, my heart sunk into its place of defeat. There was no happy ending here. We did, though, have a lovely beginning and a remarkable middle of a long life together that, as a caregiver, I had both the fortune and misfortune of holding onto. Sally, like all those with dementia, had lost all sense of the wonderful life we had shared.

After the celebration of our sixtieth wedding anniversary and then Sally's eighty-seventh birthday, I visited her almost daily at BrightStar. I wanted to be with her even as she became increasingly confused, her strength weakening, and her heightened agitation and anxiety ever more present. I wanted to be with her because I felt my presence would reassure and comfort her as she faced the agonies of her life coming to an end. I also wanted to be in regular touch with the BrightStar staff for their ongoing assessments of Sally's condition—her patterns of eating, sleeping, her mood, and her interactions with staff and other residents. Witnessing and being with Sally as she slid slowly into the darkness of death became my daily way of life.

People suffering from dementia who are unable to exercise their right to die must live out their lives until the dementia finally overwhelms them. What a sad way of having to endure the end of a beautiful life. And for loved ones to witness this? I have to wonder if there is a more bitter heartbreak. No one should have to suffer as Sally did, and no caregiver should have to witness their torment.

When I visited Sally on a Monday afternoon in early February, her on-staff caregiver had just put her down on her bed after having walked her about and engaging in completing a puzzle with her. Every so often Sally would try to sit up even though she was tired and needed to rest. Unfortunately, she couldn't drift off to sleep. When I sat beside her to console her, she gripped my arm so tightly that later I had trouble extracting myself from her grip. This led me to wonder, painfully, what kind of internal agony she was experiencing. Were her cries of wanting to die the same as they had been over the past year? Yes, but they were more frantic. Her tight grasp on my arm seemed to be coming from someone in desperate fear. Her inability to experience deep and prolonged sleep certainly made her suffering worse.

I disagreed with the view that Sally's cries about wanting to die were evidence of her advancing dementia. In my view, Sally, *despite* her dementia, retained her strongly held view about how she wanted to die. She had been very clear and lucid about this as evinced by her early advocacy of right-to-die legislation, which I had been witness to. In this she had demonstrated once again her long and continuing commitment to the right to die. Up to the end, she spoke her mind.

Sally's Approaching Demise

Knowing that Agrace nurses had talked about making comfort-care medications available for Sally indicated that they saw something I could not see, namely, signs of Sally's approaching death. I was too preoccupied with Sally's day-to-day ups and downs to see some of what they saw. I realized little or nothing could be done now to improve the quality of her life except to medicate away any pain she was experiencing. I knew that Sally did not experience the quality of life I would want for her. And she certainly wouldn't experience the kind of death she had hoped for herself—that we both had hoped for. If only she could have had a doctor, nurse, or even me available to administer a fatal medication, which would have been possible if her right to die had been legally recognized in state law.

What struck me was how Sally's crying out, wanting to die, and her not being able to settle down or rest might be part of her expressed desire to "be" elsewhere and that she was in fact, despite her dementia, ready to die. And who wouldn't be? She was ready to "go home."

The Agrace nurse who checked on Sally at least once a week noted to me that Sally did not yet have the Agrace comfort medications, and she asked for my permission to order them. I told her to go ahead. These medications would provide a low dosage of morphine every three hours as needed for pain and Levsin every two hours to dry secretions from Sally's mouth. The nurse told me that morphine was great to have available in case of a pain crisis in the middle of the night. Typically, these comfort care medications are used closer toward the end of life, but in Sally's case, they seemed to be needed before then.

A week later, when I arrived at BrightStar, Sally was in bed, sobbing. Seeing her crying was most depressing, and I wondered if this was another indication of her knowledge of her impending death. The caregiver tried to redirect her behavior but without success. Diverting a person from sobbing and what might be causing that sobbing—in this case Sally's desire to die—was impossible. I sat down beside Sally to help. She continued to plead with me to help her, saying she was dying. Again, her clinging so tightly to my arm frightened me. I was frightened because Sally had never sobbed like this, either before or after the onset of her dementia diagnosis. As far as I could tell, nothing else had changed to trigger this output of deep emotion. Again, my heart broke, for there was nothing I could possibly do to hasten her demise.

By this time, she was receiving a double dose of Clonazepam at 8:00 p.m. and nothing at 5:00 p.m. Though this change increased the risk of her falling, I indicated this was a risk we had to take if we hoped to decrease her suffering and, in that way, improve the quality of her life. I reviewed with the BrightStar nurse my desire that nothing be done to extend Sally's life. I went over Sally's end-of-life documents; they indicated no heroic measures were to be taken to extend her life, and no medications except for pain relief were to be used to combat pneumonia and urinary tract infections or any other medical problems. The nurse was in complete agreement with Sally's wishes and also mine as Sally's Durable Power of Attorney for Health Care.

The nurse asked me how I was responding. I said I had expressed my concerns to Sally and explained that we were all doing our best to ensure she was not suffering any pain. I also told Sally that I was working with the nurse to make sure nothing, in accordance with her wishes, would be done to prolong her life. When asked whether and how I responded to Sally's cries for help in dying, I told her I would like to help but could not because doing so would be illegal and I could face charges of murder if I did so. Sally had accepted that explanation too.

A Glimpse of the Old Sally

On another visit to Sally a few days later, she had been sleeping but was gradually waking up. Instead of wanting to get into her wheelchair, she preferred to lie in bed. I brought some good news, namely a new cord for her radio as well as a new CD of hymns sung by the Mormon Tabernacle Choir. With this news, she sat up and wanted me to sit on the bed beside her, something I was happy to do. To my surprise, she wanted a kiss from me and said she hoped I had a piece of chocolate for her. I did have two pieces, one for each of us. All in all, our time together was sweet, and surprisingly, she had no objections to my leaving.

What I most appreciated about that visit was seeing the old Sally I knew showing through the fog of her dementia. Other friends told me about the often-touching behaviors of individuals dying of dementia. This seemed to be such an example, as if Sally was speaking from her inner self, and it was of great comfort to me. However, the variability of her behavior showed up several hours later when she was getting her noon medications. The nurse told me later that Sally was not in a pleasant mood at all. She was insistent on "getting out of here," and it took ten minutes to get her to agree to take her pills.

When I visited Sally on Valentine's Day, she sat on her bed calling out, "Help me, help me, I'm dying, I'm dying!" As I sat beside her, she held my wrist in her usual tight grip. She was so agitated I couldn't help her to settle down. When I presented her with my two valentines she showed only moderate interest in them. Her weakened eyesight made them difficult to read; nor could she enjoy their graphics and language. However, she eagerly accepted the chocolate I'd brought with me.

Hearing her cries for help but being unable to do anything to help her proved to be distressing. To think that we had for so many years made it a point to help each other, and we'd always done it so joyfully, but now there was little or nothing I could do. How sad. But as we all know, the approach of death cannot be anything but sad.

About this time, Martha sent a note that read: "The longer this goes on, the more heartbreaking it gets. Poor Mom, stuck in some kind of purgatory. She knows she's dying, she wants help, but she can't escape—it's really tragic. And it must be awfully hard on you. I agree that her quality of life is poor, despite the heroic efforts that you, Agrace, and the people at BrightStar have made to try to keep her comfortable and ease her suffering. It's sounding like there is not much more that anyone can do to get her anywhere close to happy or even a neutral state. What a shame. I really do think that death will be a kind fate for her, and I'm hoping she won't have to suffer through this unhappy existence too much longer. I'm sure you feel the same, probably more so. When the end comes, it will be a blessing, as Grandma used to say. Your loving and generous intentions are seen and appreciated by everyone around both you and her. Hang in there, Dad. We love you. Love, Martha and Ellen."

Approaching the End of Life

When I visited one day, she was lying on her bed. I sat down beside her and bent over to give her a kiss. As I did that, she grabbed my jacket sleeves and held tightly. Again, because she also held my wrist in a vice-like grip, I had great difficulty peeling off her fingers to get away. This behavior gave me another indication that Sally must know she was dying or would soon be dying. Yet she clung to me, asking me for help to die with dignity.

The Agrace social worker shared her certainty that Sally could no longer participate in many of BrightStar's activities. She thought that the various treatments, appointments, and programs precipitated more anxiety for her, and the burdens began to outweigh the benefits. She said the staff would focus on efforts to keep her comfortable and content. She "thanked me for being absolutely the most wonderful husband and advocate for care that Sally could have ever asked for."

Later that day, Ellen informed me she was driving up late that afternoon to visit her mother and would be with us the following day until early afternoon. Ellen was also anxious to meet and visit with the nurse, so I set up a meeting for her.

Ellen reminded me that on her recent visit to Sally, her mother did not recognize her and said very little to her. Even Sally's "Help me, help me!" cries quieted down, but my Sally was persistent in letting me know she wanted help. Help to die. Help to let go. I told Sally that I loved her, but there was nothing I could do. When the BrightStar nurse asked me if I would have helped Sally die if the doctors, nurses, psychiatrist, and others had said, "Yes, she is asking for help to die, and you should help her do so," I gave the nurse my answer. While I would have liked to help, again, I probably wouldn't have agreed to do so because of the legal consequences. I could see it now: a local newspaper headline screaming out "Eighty-seven- year-old economics professor convicted of murdering his demented wife."

Sally's belief in her right to die would have called me to assist in her death. To do that I would have had to make advance preparations and then carry out the deed in her assisted care living room. But bringing about her death would have required medical knowledge I simply did not have. Nor did I have whatever concoction was needed to bring about her death. The whole experience was so surreal but this is the sad situation we find ourselves in today. Clearly, all of us should be pressing for right-to-die legislation so that others may be spared the agony Sally suffered and that I suffered as well.

Toward the end of the last week of February, the nurse told me Sally would soon die. Sally was more tired, slept more, didn't want to get out of bed and was less able to propel herself about the room. These were reliable signs that her life was coming to an end, along with her suffering. She wanted to die a quiet, peaceful death in keeping with her views on death with dignity and the right to die. It was also a favorable sign for me because it would end her long years of suffering from dementia. It was also a sad sign because it would mean the loss of my loving wife who, though impaired by dementia, would soon be departing even more fully from our long life together.

Sally gave us all the signs that she was departing this world. She was, in her own way, fulfilling her destiny and right to die. They had been telling me that she was physically strong and all her vital signs good, yet here she was growing steadily quieter and weaker.

Bittersweet Moments

I regularly brought Sally pieces of Ambrosia dark chocolate that she quickly devoured, and it was in this way that I could still make contact with her. She usually, though not always, thanked me. When she did, she whispered, with a beautiful smile on her face, "You're wonderful, you're wonderful, I love you." This was most comforting to me because it indicated she still recognized me.

On another visit several days later, Sally sat in her wheelchair, working with her companion caregiver, putting together a simple jigsaw puzzle. Sally moved her arms and hands slowly as she put the puzzle pieces in their proper spaces. When I gave her a piece of chocolate, her arms and hands moved in the same slow motion as she brought the chocolate to her mouth. This change broke my heart.

When I arrived, Sally often held tightly to the arm of her companion caregiver who sat next to her. Sally's eyes looked my way, but that was the only notice she gave me. Soon she would talk a bit, hesitantly and in a whisper. I could barely hear her even though by then I had moved to sit beside her on the bed. I gave her a piece of chocolate that she ate immediately. She told me again how wonderful I was and how much she loved me. I said the same thing to her and then gave her a hug and kiss as I left.

On Friday, I learned that Sally was no longer taking any food or liquid. This meant her body was shutting down, and she could be expected to die within the next week or so. What remained unclear was whether this development was a conscious choice made by Sally or a change resulting from her dementia. The staff and I had never talked much about the possibility of Sally stopping her eating to accelerate her death.

I believe dementia dictated her eating, but this is something I can never know for certain. Inwardly, I was cheering because what she was doing would terminate her life more quickly than if she continued to eat and drink. At the same time, I was reluctant to see her undergo the pain of starving herself to death. All I could hope for was the administration of sufficient medications to offset whatever pain she was experiencing.

What does this mean for you, the reader? As you approach the end of life, pray it is not because you suffer from dementia. But if you do, I hope you and your Durable Power of Attorney will have made clear your preferences about when and how you want to die. You should do this anyway so there is no possibility that efforts will be made to extend your life when there is no longer any good reason to live. I know this may sound harsh, and you may have religious reasons for stating your preferences differently. Above all, do something now to spare yourself some of the inevitable discomfort of dying.

As for myself, I have made out all my end-of-life documents. I hope that when my time comes, Wisconsin will have enacted right-to-die legislation. But if not, I hope that somehow I can have access to a magic potion that will permit me to die a quiet and dignified death.

Over the first weekend in March, Sally became even quieter and less responsive. However, she did reveal some of her old spirit, perhaps realizing this might be her last chance to say goodbye. Her companion caregiver that day was a smart and lively nursing school student. Later that afternoon, I found it difficult to write an account of my visit with Sally because it was such an emotional experience for me. I contacted the caregiver who had been involved in our conversations, asking her to write an account of my visit. She did, and I quote her briefly here: "After Lee arrived, he greeted Sally with a kiss on her lips; she returned his kiss as he bent over her face. When Lee asked if she wanted a surprise, she nodded yes. With that, he pulled out a small box of candy and offered her a piece; he said it was ambrosia, her favorite. She chewed on it slowly. With that she said, 'Thank you. You are wonderful. I love you."

After a bit more conversation with Lee, Sally seemed to tire. Finally, Lee left. After that, I sat next to Sally, holding her hand as I chatted with her. She looked so happy. Soon she tired and drifted off to sleep. With that, I left. What a touching experience to see how much Lee and Sally loved each other."

I will always treasure the longer account of my visit, one that proved to be my final visit while Sally retained consciousness.

The End Arrives

When I arrived early Monday afternoon, Sally was in bed with her eyes closed. Her caregiver told me that Sally had been quiet and unresponsive. Arriving with my usual supply of chocolate, I thought I could rouse her. When I sat beside her and greeted her, she did not respond. Nor did she answer when I asked if she wanted a piece of chocolate.

I took a piece of it and touched it to her lips. I wanted so to arouse her, to hear her say once again how wonderful I was and how much she loved me. But her lips did not move and her eyes did not open. I pulled back the piece of chocolate and ate it on her behalf. I finally realized that Sally was in the end stages of the long, slow process of dying.

This will be a time of contradiction, love, longing, holding on, and letting go, for you as well. There is no one way to let go of a loved one with dementia, but let go we must. Like me, you may not want to truly grasp the reality that your loved one is dying. But you must face it, and you must learn to live with it. However, you can comfort yourself while doing this by drawing on the many good memories gathered from the years of your shared life together.

When I returned to my apartment on Wednesday, March 9, I found a phone message from Ellen. She had driven to Madison that morning to have one last visit with her mother. I immediately phoned Martha, who said Ellen had already phoned her. I urged Martha to come to Madison as soon as possible because her mother was dying. Martha would arrive the next afternoon. Before leaving for the airport to pick Martha up, I visited Sally and spoke with the BrightStar nurse. She was worried that Sally was likely to die before Martha arrived.

This, too, is a profound experience for us, one that is out of our control. Most loved ones want to be by the side of the one who is dying, but due to distance and other factors, you may not be able to do that. As I finish this chapter, COVID-19 hinders this scene for countless families across the globe. Many individuals are dying alone, without loved ones by their side. The only solace I can give is that death finally arrives when it does and waits for no one.

Sally died that afternoon at 3:30 p.m. Martha and I arrived from the airport at 3:45 p.m. Sally died a quiet death. I was at her side most of the morning as she slowly weakened and her breath became shorter and more labored. I had to leave for the airport and could not be with her when she quietly took her last breath and died.

We fought a long fight together for the right to die with dignity, a right that was not granted her. I do believe that there was great peace for her in her last moments. Even though she did not take a bite of the chocolate I placed on her lips, she tasted something sweet. Sometimes that's all any of us can experience—a slight touch of something sweet that has gone and will never return.

Together, Martha and I spent some time in the room with Sally. The end had finally come.

Late that evening, I sent an email to family and friends that read: "Sally died peacefully about 3:30 this afternoon, Thursday, March 10, 2016. She was not in pain. Her heart and breathing finally stopped. She died just a couple of minutes before Martha and I arrived from the airport where I had picked Martha up. BrightStar, along with Agrace Hospice Care, did an excellent job of taking care of Sally over the past week and immediately after she passed away. At the moment, there is not much more to say. Love to all of you. Lee."

Chapter 11

GRIEVING BUT CELEBRATING LIFE IN THE MIDST OF IT

WHEN SALLY'S DEATH approached and I wondered how I would respond to it, I thought about my past experiences of grieving for loved ones.

I did not experience much grief when my parents died. As discussed before, my dad was eighty-two when he died in early 1972 after a series of small strokes. He passed away quickly and quietly. Grieving for him proved difficult because his life came to a natural end after he lived a full and interesting life. My mom died in 1993 at age ninety-six. While living in a lovely retirement home, she fell and broke her hip. Quickly hospitalized, her hip was replaced, something that would never be done now for a person her age. Because she lacked upper body strength, she could not manage the necessary rehabilitation and died soon afterward. It was a blessing when she finally passed away.

My older sister, Phyllis Hudry, died several years ago of congestive heart failure at age ninety-one. She was under the care of her daughter. Three years earlier, I visited her in Missouri for several days and could see how she was failing. Nothing could be done to lengthen her life. Every effort was made during her final days to minimize any pain she may have felt. Again, it was difficult to grieve actively for her.

My feelings after two other family deaths proved to be quite different. One occurred in 1961 when my thirteen-year-old nephew, John Hudry, died tragically in a neighbor's swimming pool. He was such a smart, young boy. Even now, more than sixty years later, thinking about his death brings tears to my eyes. Whether grieving sessions would have helped me, had they been available, is difficult to say. My sister would certainly have benefitted because she never recovered from the tragic loss of her only son.

The other untimely family death occurred in November 1943, when a War Department telegram arrived with word that our older brother, Jim Hansen, had been killed in action in Italy. He was a forward observer for an artillery battalion and was hit by enemy gun fire while securing a better position to observe and direct fire against a formation of advancing German tanks. His death was hard to accept. Now more than seventy years later, I still choke up thinking about him, too.

In reflecting on grieving, I believe the circumstances of death shapes how one grieves. In the cases of John and Jim, it is possible to visualize, even if imperfectly, the terrible circumstances under which they died. More important, each of them had many years of life before them. These considerations made their deaths much harder to understand and intensified my sense of grief.

My Reactions

As Sally approached death, I did not believe I would need grief counseling. Oakwood's social workers had already reached out to me, as had those from Agrace Hospice Care. Nor did I believe I needed any pastoral care from Oakwood Village or our own First Unitarian Society.

My situation may have differed from that of others due to Sally's slow, decade-long decline. I knew from the beginning there were no cures for dementia. I knew she would experience declines in her cognitive skills and eventually decreased mobility. The slow pace of her decline made it possible to think ahead about what kinds of care she would need later on. As well, I understood we would need to move out of our house and into a retirement home that provided assisted-living memory care. I knew it would be impossible to predict when she would die.

I suppose that throughout this decade-long period, I may have grieved at a slow and steady pace but without fully realizing it. Consequently, I didn't experience the overwhelming grief I might have felt had Sally died suddenly or at a much younger age, unimpaired by dementia. As an Agrace grief counselor expressed it, "So many caregivers experience a low simmering grief throughout the caregiving journey and a much less intense grief when the death actually happens." Indeed, the Alzheimer's Disease Association reports a recent survey indicating that over 70 percent of dementia caregivers experienced a sense of relief when their loved ones eventually died. I suppose, in my case, I derived some small comfort from the fact that Sally's wish to die had finally been granted.

Unlike a sudden death, spouses of people with dementia experience what can be described as "ambiguous loss." Though this term applies most clearly to kidnappings and people who go missing, it can also be used to describe the experience of dementia caregivers while in their caregiver roles. Their loved ones are not dead, but neither are they the people they once were, although sometimes they may be as lucid as they once were. At other times, they may be confused and no longer aware of who they once were. This is so often the experience reported by caregivers.

Keeping Busy

The life I continued to maintain as Sally's dementia worsened made her death easier to accept and thus reduced my grief. Throughout these years, I continued to be actively engaged in professional and social activities that kept me busy and provided an informal measure of support. I maintained longtime contacts and lunched regularly with several groups of retired faculty members. I participated in two book-discussion clubs, one that celebrated its twentieth anniversary in October 2015. I remained involved in academic freedom issues and campus diversity programs. I continued my research and writing, including dozens of op-ed essays and letters to the editor in both campus and city newspapers on racial-ethnic diversity plans and programs.

Added to this was my regular exercise regime that involved brief exercises every morning in my apartment, hour-long sessions walking in a warm-water pool three times a week, a once-a-week strength training session, and an hour-long session with a personal trainer to relax my tight muscles.

Perhaps most important was this book: my long-term writing project about Sally and her dementia. It chronicles the onset and progress of her dementia, describing and monitoring the care she received and dealing with her eventual decline and death in March 2016. Through my ongoing interaction with her caregivers, I learned a great deal about caregiving, much of which is reflected in this manuscript.

Throughout, I have had the enormous good fortune to be able to keep myself occupied doing things I enjoyed doing: regularly visiting Sally, participating actively in Sally's care and, since her death, reflecting on life and death. As a consequence, I have not had much unoccupied time to grieve Sally's decline and death.

Not that watching Sally's decline was easy. Early on, I became acutely aware that we could no longer enjoy the activities that provided so much satisfaction and stimulation throughout our married life. As Sally became more confused and her memory spottier, we could no longer carry on the stimulating conversations we had so enjoyed. These changes greatly saddened me, but they did not seem to have the demoralizing effect on me that has been experienced by other people I knew.

I don't believe that what happened indicates any lack of love and respect for Sally. Instead, it reflects what I recognized as the inevitability of death, something we had both talked about extensively long before the first signs of dementia appeared. Sally had thought even more than I about end-of-life issues. As mentioned earlier, she had joined the Hemlock Society back in the early 1980s and wrote a short booklet on death and dying and organized a day-long workshop on the topic at the First Unitarian Society. She already believed people should have the right to die.

My Reactions

If there is any regret, it is that Sally had to suffer so much. She realized this was a potential problem, and we agreed that neither of us wanted any heroic measures applied to keep us alive. Had she been able to act on her preferences, she would have opted to die when she'd first entered assisted-living care in April 2013. The problem: There was no legal way to do this. Instead, one must face the inevitability of death even though quality of life might be totally lacking.

When Sally died, I felt deep sadness, but the jolt of her death was ameliorated by the long time it took in coming. The real trouble I had as she neared death and shortly afterward was telling people about her condition and subsequent passing. Regularly, I choked up when friends asked me about her. I simply could not say anything. Speaking about her proved to be much too painful. Hence, I remained speechless. It took almost a month before I could finally speak about her death. By then I had recovered from the immediate shock of it. Today, I have little or no difficulty talking about her death, just as I had no difficulty talking about her slow decline during the three years she received institutional care.

What I savor are my many memories of her, particularly her last words to me: "You're wonderful, I love you," which accompanied her beautiful "goodbye" smile, as recounted in chapter 10.

Grief Counseling

Several weeks after Sally died, I saw an Oakwood announcement about the start of a weekly series of four grief sessions. At first I was going to bypass this opportunity, but then I decided I should attend, if for no other reason than to find out how these sessions were conducted. I also thought that by attending I would pick up some useful information that would help me with writing this book: chronicling Sally's life, her career, her slide into dementia, the institutional care she received, and finally, her passing.

A gifted grief counselor from Agrace Hospice Care led these sessions; she was assisted by Oakwood's two social workers and its chaplain. Nine residents—four men and five women—attended, all of whom had lost their spouses within the previous couple of months. At the first session, the leader provided helpful background information on the process of grieving. She then skillfully drew out from all of us attending our stories, concerns, and how we were reacting. The stories told were most interesting, and they varied widely.

In each subsequent session, the leader introduced us to additional information on the grieving process. Comments from participants described their feelings and how they were adjusting. By the final session, everyone seemed far more comfortable talking about their losses than at our first meeting. These sessions clearly helped the grieving individual, but so did the passage of time. How everyone dealt with their grief in the year that followed would be most interesting to know.

What were my own reactions to these sessions? I am happy I decided to attend because I learned so much and came to see how people's grief differs depending on their particular situations. The people attending who seemed to experience the greatest grief turned out to be older, female spouses who had been heavily dependent on their husbands to perform many of the responsibilities that go along with marriage. When their husbands died, most spouses found themselves incapable of coping with many decisions they had to begin making so they could continue their lives. Of course, the same is true for many men, except that all four men seemed to be adjusting reasonably well. Based on what I have heard from others, husbands do tend to adjust more rapidly and easily than do wives.

After this experience, I now appreciate the value of grief sessions, and I see the importance of offering group grief sessions. I would certainly encourage everyone who has recently lost a spouse or some other loved one to take advantage of these sessions.

Celebrating a Life

Sally and I had long talked about how we wanted to be recognized after our deaths, though neither of us laid out all the details. Our remains would be cremated, and our ashes spread by our daughters in favorite yet-to-be-determined locations.

We each wanted celebration-of-life ceremonies rather than traditional (to me) funerals. We wanted those celebrations held in the First Unitarian Society Landmark Meeting House we'd attended since our 1965 arrival in Madison. We wanted our senior minister, Michael Schuler, to conduct these ceremonies, and we wanted them to embrace tradition, have uplifting music, readings of favorite poems, and tributes from family members and friends.

We wanted those attending to have opportunities to greet one another and family members. Equally important, we wanted our obituaries to describe what kind of people we were and our major interests and accomplishments.

The Celebration Program

Arrangements for the celebration-of-life ceremony moved forward. Setting a date depended on the availability of both the minister, Michael Schuler, and the First Unitarian Meeting House. Saturday, April 30, from 1:00 p.m. to 3:30 p.m. was available. I met with the minister to discuss the general configuration of the ceremony—the music, the poetry, the speakers, his comments, and the printed program.

Within a week, we had the program firmed up. It would include one of Sally's favorite hymns, "To Be a Pilgrim," with words by John Bunyan and the musical arrangement by Ralph Vaughn Williams. It would feature one of the Unitarian Society's accomplished soloists singing the beautiful "Pie Jesu" from one of our favorite pieces of music, Faure's *Requiem*. Five of Sally's favorite poems would be read, two by each of my brothers, and one in closing by the minister. Tributes would come from our two daughters, our four grandchildren, and four of Sally's friends. The program would be printed on a folded 11 x 17-inch sheet of buff paper similar to that used for regular church services.

Identifying people of Sally's generation to offer tributes proved to be more difficult than I expected. Many had passed away, and others had moved elsewhere to be nearer their children. However, a longtime English Department colleague from Madison Area Technical College readily agreed to speak and so did a retired geography professor with whom we shared Saturday morning coffee and conversation for many years at the State Street Starbucks Coffee Shop. He agreed to write a statement but said that because of his age and infirmities somebody else would have to read it.

Recruiting the other two speakers proved to be surprisingly difficult. One dear friend said he simply could not do it because he would break down and cry midway through his comments. The spouse of a close colleague and a longtime social friend of Sally's agreed to write a statement but said her stage fright would prevent her from mounting the podium and presenting it. I reassured her, saying the minster could read it for her. I then contacted another longtime friend of ours, an articulate admirer of Sally, who could do a fine job, but he told me he, too, freezes up in front an audience and would have to decline. I went back to him, asking if he would write a statement the minister could read. He agreed, thus completing the program.

All four grandchildren expressed an eagerness to attend the celebration and to offer their tributes to their Nana. They performed beautifully and offered keen insights on their grandmother and the effect she'd had in shaping their lives.

Because I didn't want speakers to go on and on, as speakers often do on occasions like this, I gave each one a strict word limit for their comments. To my surprise, they all adhered to their limit. As a result, the ceremony lasted exactly one hour, as I'd hoped it would.

I asked the minister to announce at the close of the service the availability of refreshments in the building's loggia. Three of Sally's favorite foods would be served: Danish kringle from Racine, Wisconsin; chocolate-chip cookies prepared at a local bakery; and Fanny May chocolates. This announcement brought smiles to many faces, particularly to friends who knew Sally and her love of chocolate.

Approximately 125 people attended the celebration-of-life gathering. As many as thirty of them came from Oakwood Village, even though most of them had never met Sally. Others included Sally's teaching colleagues, First Unitarian Society friends, Shorewood Hills' neighbors, plus other friends from the Madison community.

The celebration brought together my two brothers, our two daughters, our four grandchildren, and several nieces and nephews. Since many of them had either not met each other or had met only fleetingly, the weekend ended up serving as a wonderful family reunion.

The Saturday afternoon celebration gathering went smoothly and was deeply moving. Any number of people after the gathering and since then commented on how much they enjoyed the program. Several said it helped them begin thinking about how they might fashion their own celebration-of-life ceremony. (Please see the epilogue, The Remarkable Sally Hansen, for the obituary and more information on Sally's extraordinary life.)

Part V

Specifics of the Right to Die

"Untitled" by Iefke Goldberger

All of a sudden it was enough;
As the old painful year died down
To a hesitant ... stop,
There was a moment for reflection—
For looking back with a fading smile
From the wreck of a marked body—
At the good things life has to offer:
Companionship, talents, wit, love
The magic of nature, hard work
The joys of being creative.

With the door of this world ajar,
Hope slipping away with each heart-beat
What else could be done but to give in,
Accept defeat with regret,
Follow the piper's elusive tones
While boldly surrendering the body?

Chapter 12

A RIGHT TO DIE FOR THOSE WITH DEMENTIA

ONE OF OUR MOST fundamental rights is the right to control our own minds and bodies. This means the right to declare that when, because of advanced dementia, we are no longer in full control of our minds and bodies, our prior wish to terminate our lives will be honored. When we are no longer the person we once were, our wish to end our lives should not be prohibited by the views of the medical profession (particularly state medical societies), religious leaders and their followers who believe in the sanctity of human life, and/or legislators whose responsibilities include serving the public interest rather than special-interest groups. Individual liberty, in this case control over one's mind and body—and life itself—should be honored to show respect for human dignity and individual autonomy.

This fundamental right to control our own minds and bodies is a challenge we should all embrace. We can take heart from the proponents of death-with-dignity legislation who labored for many years before the state of Oregon enacted its groundbreaking death-with-dignity legislation. Their success has stimulated ten other states and the District of Columbia, together containing 20 percent of this country's population, to enact essentially similar legislation. The success of this movement owes much to the hard work of death-with-dignity supporters, combined with the evidence and arguments they mustered to win public support for a way of death that so many people believed in and eventually came to understand and advocate for.

When discussing a Dementia Right-to-Die Directive, we need to elaborate on the right to die. To do so, we start with a draft of a Dementia Right-to-Die Directive. Legislation would authorize a directive of this kind that, when properly executed, would become a part of a person's Advanced Medical Directive (which you may find at the end of this chapter).

THE RIGHT TO DIE concept includes a distinctive path that gives practical meaning to our right to die. These include the Right to Specify *how* we want to die, the Right to Determine *when* we want to die, the Right to Terminate our lives by indicating *who* has the power to do so, the Right to Expect Meaningful Legislation establishing the right to die, and the Right to Advocate for the right to die.

THE RIGHT TO SPECIFY means that individuals have a right to express their wishes about how they want to die—painlessly, peacefully, quickly, and with dignity—if in later life they suffer from advanced dementia. One's Durable Power of Attorney for Health Care has the right to then implement these *expressed and specified* wishes.

THE RIGHT TO DETERMINE means that individuals have the right to indicate when they want to die if in later life they suffer from advanced dementia—when they are no longer the person they once were and are no longer able to engage in the many activities that for so long gave meaning to their lives. This preference has already been stated in writing in their Dementia Right-to-Die Directive and officially recorded. The individual's Durable Power of Attorney for Health Care will determine when the time has come to implement the demented individual's preference as to how and when that person wants to die. Difficulties could arise in determining *when* a person is *no longer the person they once were*. The Dementia Right-to-Die Directive would need to be carefully drawn to specify the traditional activities that an individual engaged in and enjoyed while at the height of his or her powers in order to determine when those activities were no longer viable for the individual to engage in. The Durable Power of Attorney for Health Care would be responsible for making this determination, to be verified by the individual's medical doctor and by the individual's principal care-advocate, who would be well acquainted with what the person could or could not do.

For a Dementia Right-to-Die Directive to become a legal document it would have to be completed by the individual. The document would also have to be signed by that person's Durable Power of Attorney for Health Care, their primary care doctor, as well as a caregiver who knows the person's stage of dementia through close and extended observation of the demented individual, and finally by two independent witnesses. This document would also have to be notarized to make it official. After that, one copy of this directive would be attached to the person's Advanced Medical Directive; another copy would be entered into the person's electronic medical records; and copies would go to the person's Durable Power of Attorney for Health Care, their primary care doctor, and their principal caregiver. Copies would also be distributed to family members as well as other designated individuals (e.g., clergy). Through this process, everyone should be clear about a dementia patient's end-of-life preferences.

The person's Durable Power of Attorney for Health Care, appointed in the Advanced Medical Directive document, should be well acquainted with the person and in agreement with their end-of-life preferences to aid them in determining when the process of terminating that person's life should begin. Before proceeding with this process, it would be best for the Durable Power of Attorney for Health Care to consult with members of the family and to secure their agreement in order to avoid later conflict. For people unable to afford a lawyer, hospitals should maintain an office that provides assistance in creating Right-to-Die Directives in the same way that many of them now do for creating Advanced Medical Directives.

THE RIGHT TO TERMINATE means initiating this process to terminate one's life under the direction of the Durable Power of Attorney for Health Care. This calls for assessing whether the individual's condition meets the criteria set forth in the Dementia Right-to-Die Directive. If it does, the Durable Power of Attorney for Health Care is authorized to obtain the needed medication to terminate the person's life. The next task is to arrange for a medical doctor, a physician's assistant, or nurse practitioner to administer this medication in such a way so as to terminate the person's life in accord with their Dementia Right-to-Die Directive, namely a painless, peaceful, quick, and dignified death. There are various methods of terminating one's life when one is suffering from dementia. In some cases, sympathetic primary care doctors assist individuals suffering great pain by administering fatal medications to them. Another means is via starvation, i.e., a person simply stops eating food and drinking liquids. To succeed, an individual must possess an ability to recognize that not eating is a means of expediting one's demise. The individual must also have the fortitude to implement this approach and an ability to discourage well-intentioned caregivers from offering them food and drink. Other methods require that individuals ingest lethal medications that may be difficult for the individual to obtain and take without the assistance of others. People assisting in what is known as suicide (sometimes called "rational suicide") can be subject to legal charges.

Finally, arrangements can be made to travel to other countries, most prominently Switzerland, where help can be obtained in terminating one's life. Most of these other methods are either too complicated to be implemented by people impaired by dementia, or they are too costly to implement, given the limited finances of so many people who suffer from dementia, especially those who are financially poor and/or without family.

THE RIGHT TO MEANINGFUL LEGISLATION gives attention to what kind of legislation is needed to implement a person's right-to-die preferences, namely legislation that describes the process of implementing the individual's stated preferences for dying. This includes safeguards to prevent abuses, exempts the Durable Power of Attorney and medical personal administering the fatal medication from any legal consequences of their actions, and does not unduly restrict the person's Durable Power of Attorney for Health Care from carrying out their duties to terminate the life of the demented individual.

Legislation needs to generate care that will offer provisions for terminating the lives of people suffering from dementia. Again, these will ideally be made available to all citizens without regard to their economic and social status. Once legalized, there can be online access to the documents needed for those who are interested. There can also be walk-in clinics at hospitals to inform people about their right-to-die opportunities, to counsel people interested in this approach, and to assist them in completing their own Right-to-Die Directives.

Right-to-die legislation must specify the process for creating the right-to-die document as well as the process for implementing it when the time comes to terminate the individual's life. Protections are required to prevent families and others who might attempt to terminate a life in order to serve their own ends or gain access to the property and other assets of their loved one who suffers from dementia. I am certain those responsible for writing this legislation can provide the needed protections against misuse. Reports on the state of Oregon's Death with Dignity program show little evidence of abuse. This evidence should help assure everyone that abuse of the Right-to-Die Directive would be minimized by careful drafting of the legislation.

Some reluctance to write such legislation is likely to stem from public reaction to death-with-dignity legislation that is sometimes described by opponents as sanctioning murder. Opposition to right-to-die legislation could well be even stronger than death-with-dignity legislation. Again, with the passage of time, we hope that such opposition would weaken and eventually disappear.

THE RIGHT TO ADVOCATE encourages caregivers to embrace the role of care-advocate. Advocacy can be on a small, close-in scale, such as getting your loved one on the right medications, to a broader advocacy such as in the rights of the Durable Power of Attorney for Health Care. Advocacy can include completing the Right-to-Die Directive, legalizing the Right-to-Die Directive, and making the directive part of a person's Advanced Medical Directive for those people who opt to complete the directive. We have an opportunity to become supporters and advocates of organizations promoting end-of-life planning. Such organizations need all the help they can get—both financial help as well as help derived from volunteers giving of their time—to educate the public about more enlightened ways of dealing with end-of-life issues.

Based on my experience, I would expect to become a strong advocate for right-to-die legislation as a way of helping others avoid the kind of death experienced by my wife. I would gain enormous satisfaction from working to improve the current and future lives of those afflicted with dementia.

As advocates, we need to be strongly rooted in our belief that right-to-die legislation extends to everyone. Readers of this book are encouraged to learn more about Death with Dignity and what the advocates of Death with Dignity are actually advocating. My goal is to help mobilize greater support for an individual's right to die.

It is also advised that you learn more about dementia as a disease, what can be done to deal with its effects, and what kinds of services are available to help caregivers. One can volunteer to help people who suffer from dementia. A person can experience enormous satisfaction in working to improve the process of those who suffer from this affliction.

There are many other actions we can take as care-advocates. One is to contact one's state legislators, alerting them to this concept of the right to die and urging them to introduce legislation that embodies the right to die for people suffering from dementia. Another is to write letters to the editors of your local newspapers describing the right-to-die concept and the importance of embedding it in state legislation. Finally, I would urge support of organizations such as Compassion and Choices, Five Wishes, and the Final Exit Network. These organizations are promoting ways to improve the quality of life for people at the end of life by advocating for more humane ways of ending life for people suffering great pain and indignity—whether it be from dementia, Alzheimer's disease, other degenerative diseases as well as more common causes of death such as cancer and congestive heart failure.

Most states now permit, if not encourage, people to sign Advanced Medical Directives that allow them to hasten their deaths by indicating their lack of desire for the application of heroic measures such as breathing tubes and feeding tubes. Without such measures, individuals are likely to die more quickly and with less pain and suffering than if these heroic measures were implemented. Most states make provision for individuals to wear "Do Not Resuscitate" bracelets, thereby giving those who wear these bracelets a direct choice in the kind of care they do not want to receive. In addition, individuals are already empowered to have their brains and bodies or the brains and bodies of their loved ones donated to advance medical research and particularly research on dementia.

In Summary

These rights empower both ourselves as advocates and those suffering from dementia. Like Sally, I have long been a strong proponent of the right to die, even more so after watching her being forced to live out her life suffering from advanced dementia. Death is a part of life that affects everyone and is something everyone should plan for. At my own age of ninety, I have completed my Right-to-Die Directive in the unlikely case I will suffer from dementia. The right to end our life and to plan for its ending, even when dementia is present, honors the sanctity of it. Below is a template for the Dementia Right-to-Die Directive.

The Dementia Right-to-Die Directive

Note: The first page of this document would indicate its purpose and provide other instructions similar to those in Advanced Medical Directive documents. No attempt is made to produce those instructions. What I provide here is a draft *of the essential language of the directive, as follows:*

I want it to be known—to my family, caregivers, doctors, and hospital officials who deal with end-of-life issues—that when, because of dementia, I am no long the person I once was and no longer able to engage in the many activities (to be listed) that made life so interesting and meaningful or when I have reached Stage Five or Stage Six of Dementia (to be described here or elsewhere in this directive), I authorize my Durable Power of Attorney for Health Care, (name the person) to declare that I am ready to die, empowering that person to obtain a lethal medication that will terminate my life and arranging for a medical doctor, physician's assistant, or nurse practitioner to administer that medication to me and ensure that my life is terminated quickly, painlessly, and peacefully.

I make this statement now, while I am competent to do so, hoping that by the time this statement becomes operative, the state of Wisconsin will have enacted legislation creating the Dementia Right-to-Die Directive, which would permit the termination of my life as indicated by my signed Dementia Right-to-Die Directive, dated (this date), following the procedures indicated in the directive.

I reserve the right to revoke this directive at any time but hope I would never attempt to do so. If I did decide to do so, I would have to do so on my own without prompting by anyone. I would also have to make this request to my Durable Power of Attorney for Health Care on two separate occasions, at least one week apart, to be as certain as possible I understood my request and what it would mean, followed by proper validation of this request (not described here).

This document must be signed and dated by the individuals named below, and after being notarized, filed with my electronic health-medical records and distributed to the other individuals named below.

Names, Signatures, and Dates of Signing for:
Initiator of Dementia Right-to-Die Directive
Durable Power of Attorney for Health Care for Health Care
Primary Care or Geriatric Doctor
Principal Caregiver
Witness #1
Witness #2
Hospital Official Charged with End-of-Life Documentation
Family Members
Notary Public and Seal Note

Chapter 13

TOOLBOX FOR CAREGIVERS

Introduction

With the advent of the COVID-19 virus, increasing numbers of people everywhere are coming to realize the fragility of human life. The virus has underscored the need for people to think deeply about end-of-life questions. Though clear-cut empirical evidence of this need is still limited, we may be witnessing the beginnings of a sea change in public attitudes toward death and dying.

Over the past several years newspapers have been filled with photos of people in hospital beds hooked up to ventilators and feeding tubes, surrounded by cloaked healthcare workers. Caskets awaiting burial are lined up at funeral homes, and scores of touching accounts exist of younger people—and not-so-young people—grieving the deaths of parents, grandparents, relatives, and friends. The regular, almost daily reports of deaths, new cases, and "hot" spots keep the pandemic at the center of our attention. To date, in the United States alone, estimated deaths from COVID-19 approach one million, and many more suffer from COVID's ill effects.

On another front, the number of people afflicted with dementia in the United States, including Alzheimer's disease (AD) and all other forms of dementia, now totals almost eight million. There are more than five hundred thousand deaths every year from dementia, including its most common type, Alzheimer's disease. Dementia deaths, now accounting for one-third of all deaths among seniors, are likely to continue increasing in the years ahead, barring a miraculous medical breakthrough that will either slow its progress or eliminate it. Caring for dementia's victims now requires the help of an estimated 11 million unpaid family members, relatives, and friends.

Despite the fact that in the United States, the number of deaths from dementia roughly equals the number of COVID-19 deaths, far less attention is given to the death that dementia all too often causes.

The unexpected devastation wrought by the pandemic, along with effective lobbying by Compassion and Choices, an organization dedicated to reducing end-of-life suffering, has led increasing numbers of states to adopt what is now called "Medical Aid in Dying" legislation, which was previously known as "Death with Dignity" legislation. This new legislation is typically modeled after Oregon's 1997 law on what was then called "assisted suicide." By the end of 2022, ten states as well as the District of Columbia had adopted some form of Death with Dignity legislation. New Mexico joined this group of states in early 2023. Other states are moving to adopt similar legislation but often with new requirements more favorable to individuals facing end-of-life crises.

Another organization, the Final Exit Network (FEN), has long sought to give guidance to people and their families on how to accelerate the death of family members who suffer from a variety of physical and mental conditions, including dementia. FEN regularly updates its guidebook, *The Peaceful Pill Handbook*, reporting on research and giving information on euthanasia and assisted suicide to the elderly who are afflicted with grave illness and also to their families and friends.

Based on a January 2021 survey, FEN reports that Americans want an option to hasten their death if faced with dementia. Most respondents (86 percent) viewed dementia as a serious problem, and many respondents (69 percent) knew of someone afflicted with it. The survey results also indicate that 41 percent believe that they should have access to a peaceful method of ending their lives if they become incompetent and lose their ability to care for themselves. Twenty-four percent of those surveyed objected to this approach.

More specifically, 53 percent agreed (compared to 15 percent who opposed), that people with early-stage dementia should also be able to stipulate that, if necessary in future, they mandate that their food and drink be withdrawn and specify that doctors keep them comfortable so they might then experience a tranquil and dignified passing.

To summarize, the effects of the pandemic, combined with the growing number of older people suffering from dementia, highlight the physical and human costs of death and dying as well as the extensive caregiving needed by seniors. These developments seem to be shifting public sentiment toward facilitating the termination of life for people with dementia and other grave illnesses. The alternative is for them to live out their days suffering from the debilitating and painful effects of this devastating condition.

Another organization, called Final Exit International is pushing aggressively for Right to Die legislation in Australia and strengthening such legislation in several other countries. Switzerland has already made provision for the Right To Die, available to its citizens but also to people from other countries who want to terminate their lives. Several additional countries are or have been considering moving toward a Right to Die approach. These are encouraging developments.

LET'S NOW TURN OUR ATTENTION to the toolbox, which has been designed for caregivers, for people with dementia, and for people who one day might suffer from it.

How to Use the Toolbox Approach

First, read over all of the tools contained in this chapter so you have an idea about what the tools cover. Realize that many of them are not relevant to your situation right now, but read them anyway. By familiarizing yourself with the tools, you'll learn what information is helpful to you now and what

information will be available to you at a later time when you need it.
2. After reading all the tools, choose the one or two that are the most appropriate for you and your current situation. Forget about the rest for the time being, otherwise you are likely to feel overwhelmed. Instead, focus on one tool at a time. Doing so will make your journey easier to begin and sustain.

3. Realize that everyone's dementia journey is different. That means that your experience will differ significantly from someone else's experience. That's OK. Don't compare your experience with anyone else's—there is no cookie-cutter approach or solution. Dealing with dementia is a matter of taking the information you learn and molding and adapting it to your own particular circumstances. This will give you the best results for you and your loved one.

4. Try to learn more about the tool you have chosen. Educate yourself as to what's involved. Access other resources—books, articles, webinars, podcasts, for example—to help you understand more about how to proceed. Talk with relatives and friends who are going through similar situations. In this way, you will gain a better understanding of what they are experiencing and how their experience might help you. Doing this will provide you with support and help you move forward on your own journey.

5. With dementia, learning is a key to navigating through the experience. So again, keep learning! When you feel you have made good use of one tool, review the tools to help you decide how to move forward. Doing this helps you become the best advocate for your loved one. It also helps you learn the necessary steps to take care of yourself through this journey, which is very important. In short: Focus on one step at a time, learn what you can, accomplish what you can, and keep learning!

TOOL ONE: INITIATING END-OF-LIFE CONVERSATIONS. This Tool calls for you to begin early discussing your end-of-life wishes with family and friends. Though many people are hesitant to discuss their future death, doing so is not as difficult as you might think, and your loved ones will be relieved to know exactly what your end-of-life preferences are. But what is the best way to facilitate this essential conversation?

Use the occasion of the death of a family member, relative, or friend to introduce into the discussion something about how you want to die and the reasons for your preference. This helps open the door to a discussion about end-of-life wishes.

2. When you fill out the paperwork for your state's Advanced Medical Directive (AMD) and select your Health Care Power of Attorney (HCPA) , use this as an opportunity to talk to your loved ones. This is an easy and natural way to bring up the topic of end-of-life care. Your AMD document must be signed, witnessed, and notarized to be valid. Copies should be distributed to your medical doctor, family members, and most importantly, your HCPA; your AMD should also be entered into your electronic medical records. Make certain your HCPA knows your end-of-life preferences and is willing—to the best of their abilities—to carry out your wishes. This occasion would also be a good time to urge other family members to complete their own AMDs, something they may not yet have done. Often, doing so has not occurred to them, or they are totally ignorant of the importance of doing so. You can educate and help them by explaining what you are doing, why you are doing it, and the important benefits of doing so.

3. For assistance in initiating end-of-life discussions, several helpful documents are available. The Aging with Dignity's document, "Five Wishes," offers a friendly, easy-to-understand approach in helping you decide on your end-of-life wishes. It humanizes the end-of-life process by posing five questions: Who is the person you would like to designate to make decisions for you when you can no longer do so? What kind of medical treatment do you want? What is the level of comfort/relief you envision for yourself? How would you like people to treat you? What do you want your loved one to know about your condition and your ongoing care? Because this document is not recognized as a legal document in every state, you will need to check its status in your state. Moreover, the Five Wishes document can be amended by inserting, in writing, as my wife Sally did, adding that if needed, she would like pain medication administered, even if it hastened

her death. Your signed, witnessed, and notarized Five Wishes document should be attached to your AMD, deposited with your primary care doctor, inserted into your electronic medical records, with copies given to your HCPA and to family members.

Compassion and Choices, another organization concerned with end-of-life issues, offers an extremely helpful document, "My End-of-Life Decisions: An Advance Planning Guide and Toolkit." This attractive and clearly presented document takes you through the steps you should consider, including the need to discuss your end-of-life wishes with your family, complete your AMD, select a Health Care Power of Attorney, decide what life-sustaining measures you do and do not want, and so on. Copies of this booklet can be obtained by contacting Compassion and Choices via the internet.

4. Again, begin thinking now about your end-of-life course and do what you can to engage family members in these discussions.

TOOL TWO: PREPARING FOR DEMENTIA. This Tool offers advice about how to prepare yourself for the possibility that you or your loved one(s) might in later years be diagnosed with dementia. Here are some things to keep in mind.

1. Facilitating one's own death is more difficult for people suffering from dementia than it is for others. Typically, people suffering from dementia are not of sound mind, and there is no easy way of determining and certifying that they are terminal, meaning they have less than six months to live. Even if "Medical Assistance in Dying" was made legal in every state, its restrictions would not allow people with dementia to exercise their Right to Die.

2. Several organizations have produced documents that allow people suffering from dementia or anticipating they might later in life suffer from dementia to indicate when and how they wish to die. To provide guidance for one's family and for that person's Health Care Power of Attorney (HCPA), Compassion and Choices has developed a helpful end-of-life document for elders suffering from dementia. Its "My End-of-Life Decisions"

booklet includes a "Dementia Addendum," a nine-page document entitled "Dementia Provision: Advanced Directive Addendum." This document asks you to indicate which of four levels of care you desire. The options range from "I want to live as long as possible" to "Keep me comfortable while stopping all treatments and withholding food and water so that I can die peacefully." Fourteen markers (or symptoms) of dementia range from "I have forgotten everything about my past but still recognize those closest to me" to the other end of the spectrum: "I am unable to leave my bed." This document gives you a wide range of choices for the care you will want as your symptoms ("markers") change. The document must be signed by the individual and that individual's HCPA, as well as by a healthcare provider and two witnesses. Though this document has no legal standing now, I recommend having it notarized because of the impossibility of predicting what kind of end-of-life legislation will be in force if and when you begin experiencing the early symptoms of dementia.

4. Recently, the Final Exit Network (FEN) announced its development of a "Supplemental Advance Directive for Dementia Care (SADD)." It includes a four-page explanation of the program, followed by a four-page "Supplemental Advanced Directive" form that authorizes voluntary cessation of Eating and Drinking. The form itself is a forceful one, instructing your surrogate, at the time of your specified "My Chosen End Point," to take legal action if necessary to stop any attempts to induce you to take food or drink because at this point, you do not want to extend the dying process. This document is to be signed by you as the patient as well as two witnesses and then notarized. Signed copies are then attached to your AMD and given to your HCPOA, your medical doctor, your end-of-life caregiving institution, and members of your family. FEN is committed to assisting surrogates in taking legal action to enforce your choice to die as described by your SADD.

5. My own "Dementia: Right-to-Die Directive" goes one step beyond any of the already-mentioned documents. It authorizes an individual, fearing they might at some later time in life suffer from dementia, to stipulate that when they are no longer the person they once were and can no longer perform the

functions or engage in the activities that gave meaning to their lives, (listing these functions and activities, such as knowing and interacting with family members, unable to maintain long-time social contacts, no longer able to drive, unable to participate in board games, etc.) their HCPA is authorized to obtain from the person's pharmacy a lethal medication that will result in a quick and painless death. The HCPA is then authorized to secure the services of a medical professional to administer that medication, with no fear of legal consequences for any of the participants: the HCPA, pharmacy, medical professional, or family.

Below is a template for the Hansen Dementia Right-to-Die Directive.

A Proposal
The Hansen Dementia Right-to-Die Directive

Note: The first page of this document would indicate its purpose and provide other instructions similar to those in other Advanced Medical Directive documents. No attempt is made to produce those instructions here. What I do provide is a draft of the essential language of the directive, as follows:

I, W. Lee Hansen, want it to be known—to my family, caregivers, doctors, and hospital officials who deal with end-of-life issues—that when, because of dementia, I am no longer the person I once was and no longer able to engage in the many activities (to be listed) that made life so interesting and meaningful, or when I have reached Stage Five or Stage Six of Dementia (to be described here or elsewhere in this directive), I authorize my Durable Power of Attorney for Health Care, (name the person) to declare that I am ready to die. Doing so would empower that person to obtain from my pharmacy a lethal medication that will terminate my life, to arrange for a medical doctor, physician's assistant, or nurse practitioner to administer that medication to me, and to ensure that my life is terminated quickly, painlessly, and peacefully.

I make this statement now, while I am competent to do so, hoping that by the time this statement becomes operative, the state of Wisconsin will have enacted legislation establishing an individual's Right to Die. I make this statement now, hoping that by the time this statement becomes operative, the State of Wisconsin's Dementia Right-to-Die Directive would permit the termination of my life as indicated by my signed Dementia Right-to-Die Directive.

I reserve the right to revoke this directive at any time but hope I would never attempt to do so. If I did decide to do so, I would have to do so on my own without prompting by anyone. I would also have to make this request to my Durable Power of Attorney for Health Care on two separate occasions, at least one week apart, to be as certain as possible I understood my request and what it would mean, followed by a proper validation of this request (not described here).

This document must be signed and dated by the individuals named below, and after being notarized, filed with my electronic health-medical records and distributed to the other individuals named below.

Names, Signatures, and Dates of Signing by: ____________________
Initiator of Dementia Right-to-Die Directive: ____________________
Durable Power of Attorney for Health Care: ______________________
Primary Care or Geriatric Doctor: ______________________________
Principal Caregiver: ____
Witness #1 by Name: ____
Witness #2 by Name: ____
Hospital Official with End-of-Life Documentation: ______________
Family Members: ____
Notary Public and Seal: ____

To take effect, my "Dementia: Right to Die Directive" would need legislative approval, still a formidable obstacle because of legal, religious. and other objections. Essentially, there is only one way to allow individuals who believe in the Right to Die to exercise control over their body and mind: legalization of the Right to Die. This is the only way to alleviate the suffering of so many people with dementia who end up living far too long, into a period when they are no longer the vibrant people they once were, deprived of their personhood, and spending years suffering from the effects of dementia while being a burden to caregivers whether at home or in a memory care facility.

Another potential roadblock to enacting such legislation is the issue of safeguarding people with dementia from abuse by family members who may want to terminate their lives prematurely. Their motive might be to gain access to the demented individual's financial and real property, or because ill will exists between parents and their adult children. I assume legislators will be able to deal with this problem by listening to citizens' reactions when such legislation is considered.

To summarize, the steadily growing numbers of deaths from the COVID-19 pandemic, combined with the less well-publicized but continuing increase in deaths from dementia, are bringing a new level of awareness to issues of death and dying. This includes not only the physical and human costs, but also the extensive caregiving required by seniors with dementia. People everywhere, particularly caregivers, are witnessing firsthand the extremely difficult lives experienced by those who suffer from dementia, the loss of dignity that accompanies dementia, and the inability of dementia sufferers to experience a painless end of life and a much-desired peaceful death. This interest in helping dementia sufferers and their caregivers is indicative of the growing awareness of dementia and related diseases. These developments seem to be shifting public sentiment toward facilitating the termination of life for people with dementia and other grave illnesses.

In view of the current situation, how should an individual proceed? I suggest that a person fill out one or more of the dementia directives and have them witnessed, notarized, entered into your medical records, and distributed to your HCPOA, primary care medical doctor, and family members. Make certain this document is attached to your AMD and other end-of-life documents.

Be certain that the individual who is your HCPA knows your end-of-life preferences and agrees to follow them faithfully. If your preferences change, be sure you discuss them with your HCPOA. If this individual is no longer comfortable implementing your end-of-life preferences, you will need to find someone else to take on that task. Otherwise, you cannot be certain that your wishes will be followed.

What none of the already-discussed documents will do is allow individuals to implement my "Dementia Right-to-Die Directive." All we can do is hope that society's attitudes toward death and dying evolve over time, bringing with it acceptance of the Right to Die for people suffering from dementia.

Dealing with dementia poses a special problem because by the time you might want to declare your wishes as to how you want to die, you may be judged not competent to do so. Moreover, there is no guarantee you can be described as terminal, meaning that you have less than six months to live, one of the criteria required by "medical aid in dying legislation."

TOOL THREE: SPOTTING THE EARLY SYMPTOMS. This Tool specifies what you should watch for and do prior to getting a formal diagnosis of dementia.

1. As your loved one ages, watch for evidence of forgetfulness and short-term memory loss that goes beyond what we often observe as people age.

2. On the internet, look for guidance in identifying the early symptoms of dementia. The Alzheimer's Association provides a wide array of information about AD and other forms of dementia. Some of this information is found in its annual report. Checking the Alzheimer's Association website may help you confirm that the changes you are witnessing are indeed the early symptoms of dementia.

3. The Compassion and Choices website can also be useful in providing information that will increase your understanding of dementia. You can also Google the words *dementia* and *memory loss.*

4. There are countless books on memory loss, ranging from personal memoirs by caregivers to books that describe memory loss and dementia. Your local library may have available a number of these books you can borrow. You can visit your local bookstore to find out what it may have available. Or you can go to Amazon and search for "Best Books on Dementia" for guidance if you want to purchase copies for yourself. I find it continually surprising how much information is readily accessible. Your challenge is to make good use of that information to aid you in dealing with your own dementia or applying it so that you become a better caregiver for a family member who suffers from dementia.

5. With respect to your interactions with a family member whose memory is slipping, be as tolerant and understanding as possible, patiently helping your loved one fill gaps in their memories and suggesting words they may have difficulty coming up with in conversations.

6. Inform family and friends of your loved one's memory loss; most likely they will have already noticed it.

TOOL FOUR: DEALING WITH THE DIAGNOSIS. This Tool details how you as a caregiver can help your loved one who is living with you at home after they are given a diagnosis of dementia.

1. Some people showing early signs of dementia may want to avoid getting a formal diagnosis, fearing it will affirm that they are suffering from dementia. In other cases, people may be relieved to learn what they've suspected all along: they do indeed suffer from dementia.

2. A person's primary care medical provider can arrange for a diagnosis. After you and your loved one meet and talk with this medical provider, it will probably be apparent that your loved one needs to be tested. Such tests usually involve a series of mental responses, physical observation, and frequently a CAT scan, along with an interview of the care-giver spouse by a social worker. When the testing has been completed and you and your loved one

are informed of the results, a follow-up visit is typically scheduled. At that point, options for treatment are discussed and a treatment plan is devised.

3. Different types of dementia may be diagnosed. The most common form of dementia is Alzheimer's Disease, followed by vascular dementia, which has a number of variants. The full list of the different types of dementia may be found on the internet, along with descriptions of their most common symptoms and expected progression of the disease. This is not a happy subject, but it is information both you and your loved one need to know.

4. When the time comes for a follow up memory check, go with your loved one so that you can learn more about the diagnosis and also answer questions the memory-care staff might want to ask you. Bring to that meeting your questions about the meaning and significance of the diagnosis. You should also inquire about the type and severity of the dementia, the particular behaviors it produces, and what if anything can be done to deal with these behaviors.

5. Write down the advice and recommendations of the doctor and social worker who performed the diagnosis. Try to make sure you fully understand the diagnosis so that you can explain it to your loved one after you return home and perhaps again at a later date.

6. Do your best to assure your loved one that you will do everything you can to care for them.

7. Consider switching from your primary care doctor to a geriatric physician if that is possible.

8. Think about what modifications may have to be made in your living quarters to accommodate your or your loved one's dementia. You may need to install additional grab bars in your bathroom, particularly in the bathtub or shower areas. Improved lighting may be helpful. You should also consider installing additional bannisters in your stairways to help prevent what could be serious falls. Scatter rugs may need to be removed to prevent tripping on

them. One of the worst things that can happen to people with dementia is to fall and break a hip or another extremity. Recovering from falls is often difficult and frequently marks the beginning of the end of life for the elderly and those suffering from dementia. Your local county aging agency can provide information on qualified individuals to undertake such work.

9. Begin exploring memory care/end-of-life facilities with the intention of getting your name on one or more of their waiting lists.

10. Work out with your family its plans for the financing and care of you or your loved one when more intensive home care or institutionalization is required.

TOOL FIVE: LEARNING MORE ABOUT DEMENTIA. This Tool directs caregivers to resources that can help them deal with their loved ones who are suffering from dementia.

1. There are numerous sources of information you can explore. Among them are the many published books on dementia as well as the literature contained in government publications and from dementia-related organizations. Lectures and meetings designed to help caregivers, along with conversations with friends and healthcare professionals you meet from time to time, are also quite valuable. For me, one of the most useful sources of information came from a free document published by the National Institute for Aging (NIA): *Caring for a Person with Alzheimer's Disease: Your Easy-to-Use Guide from the National Institute for Aging*. (Publication No. 12–6173, March 2010. Updated May 2013; this document was updated again in January 2019. Free copies can be ordered through the National Institute of Aging.) Even though this one-hundred-page booklet focuses on people with Alzheimer's Disease, most of its information is equally applicable to those suffering from other forms of dementia. The booklet describes clearly and in considerable detail the full range of issues confronting caregivers. I found this book invaluable in my caring for Sally.

2. Many commercially-published books on dementia are readily available. So are seminars, webinars, and podcasts that deal with dementia and its effects. Frequently, these events are listed on the website of your local AD office. Or they may be offered through your local hospital, or other groups concerned with dementia. So keep a watchful eye for announcements to such events. Another source of information about how to care for loved ones with dementia is provided through an organization called Positive Approach to Care (PAC), an organization headed by Teepa Snow. Here in Madison I attended several of her highly informative and immediately applicable hands-on demonstrations about how to become a more effective caregiver. She now makes her information available through a half-dozen books, CDs, and videos. You can purchase these materials, or you may be able to borrow them from your local Alzheimer's Association office, local hospice care organization, or local library. Let me note that I found Snow's approach most useful in dealing with Sally's behavior as her dementia progressed.

TOOL SIX: OBTAINING CAREGIVING HELP. This Tool directs readers to local sources of caregiving support and advocacy for people suffering from dementia.

1. Local organizations, among them public agencies on aging, often publish annually a comprehensive list of all local organizations and the services they offer to the elderly. These organizations and their services are often listed on the internet. For caregivers who need additional help in managing the care of their loved one, there are numerous home health care companies that can offer assistance for periods of varying duration, ranging from several hours a day to full time twenty-four-hour-a-day care. For example, the full range of services and institutions in south central Wisconsin is listed in a publication Journey of Aging. This journal, now ninety-eight pages in length and published twice yearly, is supported by the advertising of many organizations that deal with aging and end-of-life care.

2. Publications of this kind are especially useful when the time comes to move a loved one into institutional care. I was amazed to find out how many such institutions operated within the greater Madison area. This booklet made it easy to find these facilities and meet with their staff members to learn more about the operations of these facilities.

TOOL SEVEN: MOVING TO INSTITUTIONAL CARE. This Tool describes the process for finding an institutional care facility that offers both Memory Care and End of Life Care.

1. It is important to recognize that moving to such a facility is likely to be permanent, meaning that your loved one will probably reside there until he or she passes away.

2. Before too much time elapses, explore the available memory-care facilities in your locality and visit them to find out what services they offer. Doing so will also allow you to determine what their facilities are like and will give you some idea of the options open to you.

3. If you find a facility that is to your liking, sign up to get on the waiting list, and make whatever deposit (typically refundable) is required to do so. It is important to be ready to move when one of its units opens up, or to have an option to delay, for example, because you must first sell your house.

4. I urge that you make several visits and have an opportunity to meet the Wellness Nurse, the Life Enrichment Program Director, the Receptionist, and the Executive Director. Doing so will give you a chance to find out how the institution operates, the level of cooperation and coordination that takes place, the quality of the food, and the daily schedule of activities including mealtime, nap time, and bedtime.

5. Talking to the family members of residents can provide helpful information as you decide whether the institution you favor will be the best fit for your loved one.

Facilitating Quality Care for Family Members Suffering from Dementia: A Checklist of Information for Transitions Between Different Kinds and Levels of Care	
Information Family Caregivers Need to Provide to Caregiver Staff	**Information Caregiver Staff Needs to Provide to Family Caregivers**
✓ Contacts: family caregivers, other family members, DPAHC ✓ Details of dementia: onset, symptoms, clinical diagnosis, progression, caregiving provided, difficulties in providing caregiving, reasons for institutionalization ✓ Medical history, both physical and psychological: chronic conditions, recent conditions, current health concerns, past surgeries, hospitalizations, injuries, etc. ✓ Medications: prescription and over-the-counter, frequency of use, adverse side effects ✓ Doctors and other relevant professionals: names and contact information for personal physicians, medical specialists, psychiatrists, dentists, therapists, etc. ✓ Adult lifestyle: exercise routine, diet, weight control, alcohol consumption, personal hygiene habits, dental care ✓ Personality: general traits and patterns as well as idiosyncrasies ✓ Family details: childhood and family background; more recent information on spouse, children, and grandchildren ✓ Life experiences: educational background, career/work life, accomplishments ✓ Social involvement: volunteer activities, book clubs, church, etc. ✓ Social networks: descriptions of close friends, local relatives, children ✓ Interests: reading subjects, TV favorites, hobbies, musical tastes, arts and crafts enjoyed, etc. ✓ Food: likes and dislikes ✓ Caregiving involvement: extent of your interest ✓ Self-assessment: how important collaboration and good rapport with staff is to you	✓ Orientation to facility: contract and institutional rules, daily schedule of meals, activities, etc. ✓ Staff: description of staff members, their education and training, and their duties ✓ Contacts to answer questions about care for the loved one ✓ Providing caregiving information as needed ✓ Daily monitoring of resident's status ✓ Development and updating of Individual Service Plan, visiting physician service, hospice care ✓ Quarterly in-depth review of resident's status ✓ Access to resident's records ✓ Options as more advanced care is needed, e.g., companion care, transfer, hospice, etc. ✓ How to contact other caregivers and caregiving organizations ✓ Process of transfer from one level of care to another as physical condition deteriorates ✓ Switch to geriatric physician and to institution's pharmacy ✓ Involuntary transfer to another institution due to behavioral problems ✓ Emergency care: ambulance to emergency room ✓ Opportunity to sign Do Not Resuscitate agreement ✓ Treatment of infection: UTI, pneumonia, etc. ✓ Documents on end-of-life care, funeral arrangements, etc. ✓ Self-assessment: how important collaboration and good rapport with family members is to caregiving staff

6. Review the checklist below, which contains information that care-advocates should transmit to staff members as well as the information that staff members should provide to care-advocates when a loved one is admitted to memory care. This exchange of information will ease the transition to memory care for both you and your loved one. It will also make clear to the memory-care staff your expectations about the quality of care that will be given to your loved one. The list I developed during Sally's first several moves was most useful in managing her subsequent moves.

TOOL EIGHT: PERSONALIZING INSTITUTIONAL CARE. This Tool provides suggestions as to what you can do to gain additional attention and quality care for your loved one.

1. As soon as possible after your loved one is admitted to a memory care facility, explain to the staff your loved one's end-of-life preferences and give them copies of your loved one's end-of-life documents.

2. Post a large-print list of conversational prompts in the resident's room. This will help staff caregivers connect with your loved one. Examples of prompts are: "Tell me about yourself," "Where did you grow up?" "Tell me about your family," "Are you married?" "Do you have children?" "Tell me about them," and so on.

3. You may want to request the installation of a white board in the resident's room with photos of the resident and their family and friends to help your loved one adapt and to provide a visual "conversation prompts" for staff members.

4. Prepare a three-ring binder that provides staff members with additional information about the resident, such as their most recent employment, education, interests and hobbies, their family members, where they grew up, and where they've lived. Also list some of their likes and dislikes in food and their interests in TV and music, as well as some of their idiosyncrasies. The

purpose is to help staff members relate to your loved one and be stimulated to provide the highest level of care for them.

5. Visit your loved one as much as possible to help him or her adjust to the new living space, one that will be vastly different from the home where you cared for them.

6. Indicate to the caregiving staff your interest and concern for their new resident. Join your loved one for occasional meals. Vary the timing of your visits so you can observe the full range of care being provided. Attend meetings for family members to learn more about the memory-care staff, its facilities, and its services.

TOOL NINE: HEADING FOR EMERGENCY CARE. This Tool offers suggestions about how to smooth transitions from home care to emergency room (ER) care and in some cases, if needed, on to hospital care following an emergency room visit.

1. Find out the caregiving institution's rules and policies regarding the transfer of residents to emergency room care for health reasons and also for behavioral issues.

2. If and when your loved one is sent to the ER, ensure that the institution in which they reside provides the ER with an explanation as to why the resident is being sent for emergency room care and also who at the institution may be contacted for further information about the ER patient.

3. Make certain that the institution informs the resident's primary care doctor or geriatric doctor, and also the person's HCPA, with news of a resident's transfer to an emergency room.

4. If you are the primary caregiver, try to get to the hospital emergency room so that you can offer additional information about your loved one and the

circumstances surrounding the visit. In this instance, you should also observe/ learn what the staff is doing to care for your loved one and determine whether or not additional care, such as hospitalization, may be required.

The checklist shown earlier will help you organize what needs to be taken into account when transitioning your loved one from one level of care to another.

TOOL TEN: QUESTIONS ABOUT MEDICATIONS. This Tool deals with the confusion about the antipsychotic medication Seroquel prescribed for my wife Sally as well as concerns about other similar types of medications.
1. Find out more about what additional medications are being prescribed for your loved one by studying the medication guides that accompany the prescriptions.

2. Discuss the medications' benefits, risks, and side effects with your caregiving nurse and staff members. You can get further information from your pharmacist.

3. If any of the medications carry federal Food and Drug Administration "black box" warnings, ask your primary care doctor to explain the risks and also the sometimes underemphasized benefits of such medications, as in the case of Seroquel. "Black box" warnings indicate a medication has serious or life-threatening side effects or risks.

4 If you want more detailed information on medications that carry black box warnings, check for details on the FDA's website to learn more about the effects of such medications, including both their risks and their benefits.

5. You may need the help of your pharmacist to understand the results of the clinical trials conducted to determine the effectiveness of black box medications. The technical write-ups are often difficult to understand.

TOOL ELEVEN: COPING WITH CAREGIVER BURNOUT. This Tool offers suggestions on how best to deal with the exhaustion of a loved one resulting from what are often long months, or even years of full-time caregiving.

1. Might there be local support groups whose meetings would help alleviate the burnout of the principal caregiver?

2. If the principal caregiver for a person with increasing acute memory loss seems to be facing burnout, try to connect that individual with a local service organization that might be able to help them.

3. Can family and friends be approached about providing short-term respite care?

4. Are there local private or nonprofit caregiving organizations that provide home or companion care that will reduce some of the stress felt by caregivers?

5. If th principal caregiver for a person with increasingly acute memory loss seems to be facing burnout, try to connect them with a local service or organization that might be able to help them.

TOOL TWELVE: IMPROVING THE QUALITY OF CARE. This Tool suggests what you as a caregiver can do to improve the quality of care provided to your loved one and to other residents.

1. The most important thing you can do for your loved one after they enter memory care is to observe how it operates and what kind of care it provides. Visiting on an irregular basis and at different times of the day can be most helpful in gaining a better understanding of the quality of the care being provided.

2. It is important to become well-acquainted with the caregiving staff, and particularly the wellness nurse who works most directly with your loved one and can best answer your questions about that person's care and well-being.

3. Be diplomatic in pointing out what you see as differences in the care being provided and your understanding of the kind of care that should be provided.

4. Try to learn more about the care that caregivers can provide by consulting one of the many books and videos about caregiving.

5. Become acquainted with the family members of other residents to learn more about their experiences.

6. Try to attend all meetings scheduled by the caregiving staff so you can learn more about the institution, its staff, and the care they provide.

7. If you discover the caregiving staff is behaving inappropriately, report this to the wellness nurse and the Executive Direction, and if that fails, report it to the state's regional ombudsman. You should find posted in the corridors of memory care and skilled nursing a statement about the quality of services offered, sometimes described as a Patient's Bill of Rights, along with information about how to contact the ombudsman.

TOOL THIRTEEN: AS DEATH APPROACHES. This Tool advises what can be done to prepare for the soon-to-be-expected death of a loved one, and what may need to be done after that person's death.

1. Reemphasize to caregivers the individual's preferences for end-of-life care, as indicated in your loved one's end-of-life documents on file with the facility.

2. Alert close family members, particularly those who live far away, that they may want to make a last visit before their loved one passes away.

3. Try to prepare yourself for the person's death, recognizing that their personhood has slowly eroded over time as a result of their dementia, and that they will never be able to recover from their dementia.

4. Start preparing an obituary.

5. Speak with a funeral home about burial/cremation.

6. Decide whether to have an autopsy performed and whether to donate the person's body for medical research or dementia research.

7. Make arrangements for a funeral, memorial service, or celebration-of-life gathering. This involves selecting a site and someone to preside over the event, deciding on the overall tone of the event, determining who will speak and what music will be performed, and what refreshments, if any, will be served.

8. Think about how you might like to memorialize your loved one's life and work. One approach is to list that person's favorite charities.

9. You might also consider mailing a copy of the Service to distant friends and relatives who might not know of the person's death.

10. Prepare to undergo a period of grieving for your loved one. Find out what grieving help is available in case you need to use it. This can be done by contacting your physician or you loved one's primary care doctor, memory-care staff, hospice or hospital social workers, or your church. You may think you do not need such help, but it's quite likely you will. Meeting with other grieving family members can be most helpful in giving you perspective on your own grieving behavior.

TOOL FOURTEEN: ADVOCATING FOR DEMENTIA RIGHT-TO-DIE LEGISLATION. This Tool is designed to help you decide whether and how you want to support programs and legislation that promote the end-of-life care and wishes of people suffering from dementia.

1. Several organizations have already been mentioned, such as Compassion and Choices, Death with Dignity, and the Alzheimer's Association. Here in the Madison, Wisconsin, area we have another related but independent organization: the Alzheimer's & Dementia Alliance of Wisconsin, the Dane County agency on Aging, as well as the Agrace Hospice. All of these organizations are advocates for better end-of-life care and death with dignity.

2. You can support these not-for-profit agencies financially.

3. You can join these organizations to support their efforts to improve the end-of-life experiences of the elderly with dementia.

4. You can volunteer to work with these organizations in advancing their educational and political efforts to promote death-with-dignity legislation and dementia-right-to-die legislation in your state.

5. A number of states and counties have agencies or departments that are designed to deal with the aged and aging. Find out how you can support their efforts.

6. You can also volunteer at your local hospice to provide care for residents suffering from dementia.

7. Finally, you can lend your voice by writing letters to the editor of your local newspaper, testifying at public hearings on legislation dealing with end-of-life issues, and speaking out to relatives, friends, and neighbors on the subject of death and dying. In so doing, emphasize what we need to do to ease the end-of-life passages for members of our families as well as our fellow citizens afflicted with dementia.

A Final Word about Tools

As care-advocates we all have different experiences, depending on where we are and where our loved one lives. Services, attitudes, and resources vary, sometimes drastically from state to state and even from community to community. Overall, I had positive experiences with doctors, healthcare professionals, and caregivers. I hope you are having similarly favorable experiences.

Please take into account your personal experiences when applying the tools offered here. Make sure to check your local resources as you advocate for your loved one. Also check to find out if your area has an ombudsman program with which you can register any complaints you may have. Be assured that most assisted-living memory-care facilities are subject to surprise inspections to determine whether these facilities are complying with the rules governing their operations. These facilities want to avoid receiving any citations for fear this will make them less attractive as they recruit new residents.

Finally, it can be extremely helpful to keep a journal to record the events surrounding the care and changes in the care of your loved one. Keeping a record helped me to confront and get a better sense of what was happening to Sally and ascertain changes in her memory and well-being. Doing this also helps with remembering what worked and what did not work. I kept a record of changes in Sally's treatment and behavior. One result, of course, is this book you now hold in your hands. Again, find what works for you, but I do recommend some note keeping as a way to both channel and direct your path of care and advocacy.

Finally, recognize that you have a difficult road ahead of you as a caregiver. Learn as much as you can about dementia. Work to encourage high quality care for your loved one. And, take good care of yourself. Good luck.

Epilogue

THE REMARKABLE SALLY HANSEN—ACCOMPLISHMENTS AND OBITUARY

Sally's Accomplishments

Sally excelled at whatever she did, and she was a champion for the things she believed in. One example of this was her view of feminism, which we have touched on before but will elaborate on here. Given that feminism was such an integral part of her personality, and had been since she was young, Sally constantly sought ways to improve the lot of women in whatever way she could.

One of her proudest accomplishments occurred during her first several years in Madison. She spearheaded a successful drive to establish Madison's school lunch program, becoming known among her friends as the "school lunch lady." This meant working with the school board to organize a survey of elementary school parents, collecting and analyzing the survey results, and preparing a 125-page report for the Metropolitan Madison School Board recommending implementation of the program. Within a year, and with her ongoing help, the school board adopted the proposed school lunch program and had it operating by fall 1967.

This newly implemented program had a profound effect. Young mothers were released from the need to be home for the long, ninety-minute lunch period, enabling them to enter the work force in ways not previously possible. Sally regarded this as her modest but important contribution to the then-emerging feminist movement.

Feminism proved to be a continuing theme for Sally her whole life. No doubt her passion grew from seeds planted by her female relatives. In addition to graduating from college, several members of her female family, including her mother, had been involved in the campaign for women's suffrage, marching and carrying placards advocating for a woman's right to vote, which was finally ratified in 1920. Sally realized, based on stories she heard about that experience from her mother and several aunts, that with determination, much could be done to change the world. Her experience with the school lunch program confirmed her view that women could accomplish great things.

Based on Sally's accomplishments, her friends urged her to seek a leadership role in the League of Women Voters. Other friends wanted her to run for a position on the school board. Katheryn Clarenbach, the first chairperson of the National Organization for Women, pressed Sally to join in her efforts to expand the reach of NOW. Sally and I talked extensively about her options. In the end, Sally—and I fully agreed with her—wanted instead to resume her teaching career as soon as our daughters were further along in school.

To prepare for teaching high school English, Sally enrolled in several UW-Madison English Department courses. She loved being immersed once again in the world of literature, and she performed with distinction. She greatly enjoyed the courses taught by Professor Joyce Steward, particularly one for teachers of English. One paper she wrote for that course, "Teaching the Poetry of War," drew on her own teaching experience. It appeared in the prestigious English Journal in 1970 and received wide attention. In a graduate course on American poetry, she wrote a paper on two of Henry David Thoreau's poems. The professor's written comment on her paper was "brilliant," and it was marked "A+."

When I discovered this paper while going through Sally's files several years ago, it so impressed me that I sent it to a Thoreau scholar who then helped see it through to publication in the Thoreau Society Bulletin (2012). Although her cognitive abilities were in decline at that point, Sally was still able to appreciate her accomplishment, saying "Not bad for an eighty-three-year-old."

Teaching at MATC

The day came when Sally finally realized her ambition to return to teaching, but that teaching took a quite different form. She was not teaching top high school students but rather those on the lower end of the academic ladder, the fellows interested in learning a trade rather than the niceties of English literature. Specifically, in the fall of 1969, Sally obtained a position teaching English and Communications courses at the Madison Area Technical College, better known then as MATC and now rechristened Madison College. She remained on its teaching staff until she retired at the end of the 1992–93 academic year. Sally's willingness and ability to engage with students of all types of backgrounds and levels of education proved to be her great strength. It resulted in lasting friendships and a highly successful and rewarding teaching career.

Sally spent most of her teaching career in MATC's vocational-technical program rather than the liberal arts-based college transfer program. For many of those years, she worked with mostly young, male students fresh out of high school who wanted to learn a trade. That was a completely different world than the one she inhabited as a graduate student studying the classics, such as Chaucer's *Canterbury Tales* and Emily Dickenson's poems. However, she enjoyed the challenge of trying to reach these nontraditional, predominantly male students who were more interested in acquiring vocational skills and the good jobs that followed than bolstering their writing and speaking skills.

In the mid to late 1970s, Sally embarked on an effort to bridge the wide gap between her approach to teaching as a "word person" and the "hands-on" style of the young men she taught. During a sabbatical leave, she enrolled in a variety of "vo-tech" courses. Among them were welding, gas welding, auto mechanics, and printing. She always regarded this time as one of the most challenging and yet satisfying times she experienced in all her years of teaching.

Known as "the English teacher who had taken welding classes," her MATC colleagues continued to speak with admiration about her decision to enroll in these "core" technical classes alongside the same students she taught in the general education courses. A key observation Sally made based on this experience was that vo-tech instructors generally gave minimal instructions up-front when making assignments. Instead, they pushed their students to get started, knowing they would soon come up with questions they needed to have answered before they could proceed. This insight, which she then applied to her own subject area, allowed her to be more effective in reaching her nontraditional students.

The East Side "tech center" where Sally began teaching, across the street from the old Oscar Mayer plant, proved to be a virtually all-male environment. Most apparent was the lack of restrooms for women. Sally characterized the tech center as having a locker-room atmosphere with crude jokes bandied about and "girlie" pictures adorning the walls. She could not be intimidated by either the passive-aggressive behavior or the overt hostility she experienced, as did the one other female colleague who headed the library. Over the years, as the number of female faculty members and female students gradually increased, Sally worked hard to make the tech center a friendly environment for women. Her decision to take welding classes made a deep impact, helping to establish her credibility and toughness in the then-prevailing atmosphere of skepticism about women's abilities. Her continuing battle led to burnout. At that point in the mid-1980s, she moved to MATC's downtown campus, where there were significantly more female students and faculty members. Here she found a friendlier and gentler working environment, and soon she was truly enjoying teaching again.

Here are two letters that colleagues wrote of their time working with Sally. The first is from Mike Irwin, who taught English and supervised the student newspaper, SLATE. He and Sally got along well together; he was bright, articulate, and engaging, as evidenced by his letter below.

Dear Lee:
Though it was good to hear from you, I was both saddened by her illness and deeply reflective about how Sally and I enjoyed each other and how my own teaching life intertwined with hers at the MATC Technical Center during the early and mid-1970s. So on to my assignment, Lee, in random thoughts, feelings, and rememberings. I'll elaborate on the teamwork we pulled off during those years.

I looked forward to seeing Sally each day. She was bright and warm yet critical and tough. She spoke honestly, openly, and privately about the "old boys club," the older, often militant unionists and tradesmen who worked there before Sally arrived in 1969 and I in 1971. I think we felt a quick respect, gratitude, and inspiration in being together. Simply put, we supported each other and shared more street smarts than those old farts could ever imagine. It was accident, magic, and necessity all working together, and it brought us early appreciation of one another's values, goals, daily teaching practices and problem solving as we taught Communications and Communications Skills to one- and two-year students.

Whether in the teachers' lounge or classroom, Sally commanded respect. I did not say, "demanded." Some of the trade teachers were openly sexist. They'd say, "A woman doesn't belong out here," or "Her classes have nothing to do with our students' work after graduation." Others, having a bit of intellectual dimension, met her face to face, engaged her without sniping, and even planned and shared a project with us once a semester.

Each in our own way, Sally and I decided to enter the shop/trade world and workday. We would lock elbows with our students and their teachers, too, by God, by enrolling in trade classes for an entire semester. Sally enrolled in auto engine tune-up and later electric welding for a full semester each. I took welding, engine rebuilding (beginning and advanced), and later typesetting composition using the new-generation PC typesetters.

We were patient but inept learners. We asked questions. We asked students for help. We got dirty, learned to talk the talk ... and this last one was critical, I mean critical to our acceptance by the tradesmen. Little by little, we built writing, research, and speaking projects into work directly related to students' lab work and their futures. We slowly, slowly climbed inside their skin and experienced a dimension of worker lives present and future.

Sometimes for each of us, the classroom meetings were just plain lousy. Some loud-mouthed leader would say Sally's assignments were "bullshit." God, how she could roll with such punches. Better, I think, than I could. Over time, we figured out which trade teachers were reinforcing and even leading their students to express such attitudes. She and I would talk with those teachers, Mel Saemens, Gary Gade, Gene Hatsinger, and Paul Meister casually. We would ask their advice about a good writing or speaking project.

Once in a while, students would take us to the edge. No work was handed in. "No work, no grade, no graduation," she'd respond without skipping a beat. First we toughed this news out with the abusive, ignorant student, then we might give the same news to the student's program leader—his lead teacher.

That made "the shit hit the fan" as the teaching guys might say. The student got an unexpected shape-up-or-ship-out lecture from the trades leader or be told he'd get no associate degree or diploma but only a humble "certificate" of completion for a finished trade, but not humanities or social science work like the kind Sally and I did.

As the 1980s came on, both Sally and I got assignments at the Uptown Campus and later at Truax. We saw less of each other. Sally, as I think back now, actually became a more devoted and persistent feminist than in early days we two "literati, elite ones" were trying to survive and still honor our good students and graduate literate young men ... and eventually a few courageous women who entered the trades programs.

Last I remember, as Sally was easing off toward retirement by going to half and then quarter contracts, she helped organize and create early strategies for the Learning Center, a one-on-one help section established inside the Truax Library. Even after retiring, she sometimes came to the Learning Center to volunteer.

I missed her in those last years. You have prompted me to miss her now. I am grateful for her presence in my days as well as her integrity, fearlessness, and wit.

Thank you for giving me this charge to remember being with Sally and perhaps for a chance to grieve some for both of us.

—Mike Irwin

The second letter was written by Jean Lind, who began teaching English in the late 1970s. Through a mutual friend, Jean and Sally became very close and remained so over the years. Jean was always a strong supporter of Sally, and the same was true for Sally of Jean.

The Many Sallys I Have Known

In the summer of 1977, I met Sally's daughter, Ellen, a research assistant for Joyce Steward and me in the UW English Department. Shortly thereafter, I most fortunately met the strong and supportive woman standing behind her motivated intelligent daughter.

In 1981, when I began teaching at MATC, Sally, a teacher at MATC, became my colleague. New to MATC teaching at a community and technical college, I found Sally eager to share materials and to mentor newcomers like me. She was a force in the English Department, from curriculum work to being a powerhouse for the department's adopting a nonsexist language policy. By colleagues and students, Sally was greatly respected for her teaching ability and courage. With fearlessness, she enrolled in a welding course with young men in that program so that she could teach those same students in a way that nobody else could. She motivated them, kept them in line, had expectations for them, and because of this, they respected and worked for her. I also know that she was the favorite teacher of my neighbor's daughter—a young woman who at that time was challenging authority on every front, rebelling in multiple ways, even living in a foster home.

My deep bond formed with Sally because of her longtime dedication to women's issues. Whether as a member of the first Women's Initiative Committee, a committee developing a sexual harassment policy for the college, or a panel on Women and Aging during Women's Week, she was a solid presence and role model for all women. After testifying at a hearing for a woman student who had been sexually assaulted by an MATC teacher, I was targeted to be laid off; Sally was there for me and the student in every way—from multiple hearings to letter writing to personal hand-holding—gestures that I will never forget.

Sally's breadth in interests and intellect were always a model for me. Her connection with foreign students, teaching them and taking them into her home, spoke to a lifetime curiosity, which inspired her joy of traveling. She was an avid reader and member of a book group for as long as I have known her. And then add her bottom-line support of her two daughters, their families and partners, and, of course, her dedication to Lee, who has shown his unending love for her as she has struggled with dementia—a most unfair turn for Sally.

Whether we might be riding to Truax Campus together or meeting at Border's for coffee after her retirement, Sally and I took on the world's issues, especially if they involved feminism. I am certain that our comments disrupted more than a few readers at Border's.

I have treasured my friendship with Sally because of her unwavering commitments, sharp intellect, keen sense of humor, generosity, and warmth.

Let me be supportive in any way that I can as Sally faces the most recent challenges.

—Jean Lind

An Active Retirement

After Sally retired in 1993, she embarked on a new learning and teaching career. She regularly attended lectures on the UW-Madison campus. She also enrolled in a number of courses offered through the UW-Madison-affiliated PLATO program (Participatory Learning And Teaching Organization). She soon volunteered to teach several PLATO courses on language that drew older adults interested in lifelong learning; she found these students a refreshing change from her former students.

Sally also began teaching English as a Second Language under the auspices of the Madison Friends of International Students and did so for more than a decade. Here she worked with another fascinating group of young women who were the wives of foreign graduate students and visiting faculty members. She loved this kind of teaching and did it in creative ways. In addition to helping her students with grammar and pronunciation, she took them on "field trips" designed to get them better acquainted with the Madison area as well as to provide practical assistance and coaching with everyday tasks.

In addition, Sally came up with creative writing assignments. One of her most successful and interesting assignments required that each student write an essay comparing her own life with that of her grandmother's. Each school year was highlighted by parties at our house to celebrate Halloween, Christmas, and the end of classes in May. These were occasions of great fun and merriment as well as wonderful opportunities to promote cross-cultural understanding. Sally was at her best doing this kind of teaching.

When Sally reached a point where she found it difficult to stand while teaching because of nagging back problems, she switched to another form of teaching by serving for a half-dozen years as a Conversational Partner. This involved working one-on-one with young female students wanting to improve their English. She met them at our home once a week. She loved to converse with these students to learn more about the varied cultures from which they came. Sally maintained contact with many of these young women long after they returned to their home countries.

By fall 2010, as her dementia worsened, Sally could no longer continue her conversational partner associations. She told me that she found preparation too difficult. She could no longer maintain the flow of conversation she had enjoyed so much. Her students sensed her difficulties and tried to make their meetings useful, but soon even that was no longer possible.

Sally's Obituary

When Sally had been approaching death, I pondered the matter of her obituary, wanting it to convey what a remarkable and accomplished woman she was. In particular, I wanted it to highlight the many aspects of her life few people knew about because of her modesty.

At my urging some years earlier Sally had drafted an obituary for herself. What she produced was a bare-bones account of her life that gave no indication of the kind of person she was. I expanded it after her dementia took hold. I did further work on it after she was put on end-of-life medications a month before she died. I sent off my reworking of Sally's draft to our daughters, Martha and Ellen, so they could add their perspectives. The two of them, but particularly Martha, greatly improved the content and style of my draft.

We ended up with a beautifully written obituary of approximately one thousand words. We said what needed to be said. The obituary was published in the Wisconsin State Journal on March 20, ten days after Sally's death. I received numerous favorable comments on it. Several people who did not know Sally expressed the wish that they could have known her. Others who knew her commented on how effectively the obituary captured Sally's personality and accomplishments.

SALLY P. HANSEN: A LIFE OF LOVE, LAUGHTER, LEARNING, LANGUAGE, AND LITERATURE

MADISON: Sally (Porch) Hansen died at BrightStar Senior Living on March 10, 2016. There she reached the end of a decade-long descent into the darkness of dementia and with it release from the agitation and anxiety caused by that dreadful disease.

Sally will be remembered as a teacher, feminist, mentor, and friend. Also known as a lover of cats, chocolate, and conversation, she lived a vigorous, involved, and intellectually engaged life.

Born on January 23, 1929, in Kankakee, Illinois, to James W. and Rachel B. Chadwick Porch, Sally grew up in Detroit, Michigan. A 1951 graduate with honors from Wayne State University, she became a high school English teacher. In the summer of 1954, she completed an MA degree in English Literature at UW-Madison.

While serving as a dormitory Housefellow that summer, Sally dated W. Lee Hansen, another house fellow and a graduate student in economics. After their marriage on December 26, 1955, she joined Lee in Baltimore where she taught English at the prestigious all-girls Eastern High School. In 1957, they moved to Washington, D.C., where their daughter, Ellen, was born, and then to Los Angeles, California, in 1958, where another daughter, Martha, was born in 1960.

A series of moves took them from Los Angeles to Chicago, back to Los Angeles, and then again to Washington, D.C., before Lee's appointment in the UW-Madison Economics Department in January 1965. Sally quickly became active in the Madison chapter of the National Organization for Women (NOW), the League of Women Voters, and the Junior Great Books Program. She also resumed her intellectual pursuits in UW courses and, inspired by Professors Harry Clark and Joyce Steward, published several papers.

As one of her proudest accomplishments in those early Madison years, Sally spearheaded institution of a city-wide school lunch program. Her motivation: to enable mothers of school-age children to join the work force by relieving them of having to be home preparing meals for their children during the ninety-minute lunch period. Madison's school lunch program, begun in 1967, will mark its fiftieth anniversary next year.

In 1969, Sally began teaching English and Communications at the Madison Area Technical College. Rather than selecting the liberal arts, college-transfer program, as might be expected for someone with her background in language and literature, she chose to teach students in technical fields, who were less than enthusiastic about learning writing skills. To gain perspective on teaching these practically minded students, she spent a sabbatical year enrolled in courses on welding, auto mechanics, and printing. She used this hands-on learning to discover new ways of reaching these students and thereby earned their lasting respect.

While at MATC, Sally did much to pave the way for women who felt intimidated by the all-male, "locker room" environment then dominating the East Side Tech Center. So pervasive were gender assumptions in that era that the building had been constructed without women's bathroom facilities! Never afraid of a confrontation, Sally spoke out about issues that female faculty and students faced in this environment. She provided individual support to victims of sexual harassment and was instrumental in establishing a system-wide grievance procedure to deal with such complaints. She also mentored many female instructors, who admired her high teaching standards.

After retiring in 1993, Sally took up another form of instruction: teaching English as a Second Language through the Madison Friends of International Students (MFIS). When health problems eventually interfered with her classroom teaching, she became a conversational partner with a succession of young women, mainly wives of young faculty or graduate students from countries including Thailand, Turkey, China, Italy, Pakistan, and South Korea. She found this one-on-one teaching extremely satisfying and formed lasting friendships with these young women.

Always available for coffee at Starbucks or lunch at the old Ovens of Brittany, Sally enjoyed nothing more than a lively conversation. She was a friend to many who deeply appreciated her ability to listen empathetically and to offer support and perspective about personal and professional issues. She was also well-known for her irreverent sense of humor and her low tolerance of pomposity; she did not suffer fools gladly and did not mind saying so. Her direct (some would call it "blunt") communication style was appreciated by those who had similar thoughts they were hesitant to express. This facility also made Sally a valued member of several book groups and engaged her active membership in the First Unitarian Society and her involvement in the work of Planned Parenthood, NARAL, and the Hemlock Society (now Compassion and Choices).

Well known for her love of the English language, Sally was frequently sought out by friends and family members for guidance on grammar and usage. Indeed, even as her memory faded, she regularly corrected the grammar and pronunciation of those who cared for her, whether doctors, nurses, or assisted living staff members. However, given her erudition in this area, grounded in four years of high school Latin, she was, during her teaching career, remarkably forgiving of her students' grammatical lapses; to those completely bewildered by the apostrophe, her advice was to simply not use it at all!

Sally exhibited her lifelong love of literature by frequent quotations from the likes of Shakespeare, Wordsworth, and Virginia Woolf, as well as her extensive vocabulary. Although remarkably plainspoken at times, she was also fond of arcane words which she delighted in using for dramatic effect.

Survivors include her husband of sixty years, W. Lee; daughters, Ellen "Ellie" (Harvey) Dunham of Glen Ellyn, Illinois, and Martha (Lina Sandve) Hansen of Albuquerque, New Mexico; four grandchildren, Zachary of Portland, Oregon, Calvin of Culver City, California, Hannah of Berlin, Germany, and Tessa of Glen Ellyn, Illinois; her sister, Nancy of Woodland, California; and her sister-in-law, Judy Porch of Dearborn, Michigan. Her brother, Richard, predeceased her, as did her parents. She is also survived by nieces and nephews and grandnieces and grandnephews.

The Hansen family appreciates the dedicated and compassionate care Sally received from the staff at BrightStar Senior Living and Agrace Hospice Care. A special thanks goes to BrightStar's Nurse and Wellness Director, Robyn Shearer. Memorials may be made to Agrace Hospice Care, Planned Parenthood, and Dane County Humane Society.

AFTERWORD

Martha L. Hansen and Ellen H. Dunham

THE SHORT ESSAY toward the end of this book entitled "The Remarkable Sally Hansen" describes the mother we once knew, a woman known and loved for her sense of humor, her intelligence, her love of the English language, and her dedication to her teaching career.

How tragic it was that our highly verbal mother, who loved nothing more than a lively conversation, came to the end of her life virtually mute. Likewise, her physical activity dwindled, as did her always active and vibrant social life. The crossword puzzles she had enjoyed, the books she had devoured, the friends she had treasured – all were lost to her as she was left isolated in a world devoid of meaning and filled with fear, anger, and sadness. Adding to the poignancy of the situation was the fact that dementia was a fate our mother had long dreaded, and she had for years been a steadfast supporter of Death with Dignity.

This left us facing an agonizing irony: If Mom had been able to exercise a choice in the matter, we have no doubt that she would have chosen to end her life. Indeed, so strongly had she expressed this feeling over the years that we would not have hesitated to assist her in this had she asked. Alas, given that she was no longer legally competent to make this decision, we could do nothing to honor that long-held wish. Thus she was forced to continue to suffer until she finally, mercifully, slipped away. And so ends the story of

"The Remarkable Sally Hansen."

At the same time, another story continues, one that we feel deserves equal attention: that of The Remarkable W. Lee Hansen.

During the period of time these events took place, we, Lee and Sally's daughters, were both living elsewhere, one across the country and one abroad. Our father frequently sought our advice and kept us well informed of all the twists and turns and ups and downs of our mother's health situation; however, because he did so in such a calm, rational – even stoic – manner, we remained to a large degree unaware of the depth and complexity of the struggle he was engaged in.

Being the competent, highly intellectual, and even-tempered individual that he is, Dad never made things sound terribly alarming or upsetting; indeed, he seemed to take everything in stride and never demonstrated signs of fear or distress, much less hopelessness or despair, always simply focusing on the next problem to be solved. In an extension of the academic approach he had honed over the course of his career, he doggedly gathered data and assiduously recorded it in an attempt to take what control he could over the unpredictable events that were unfolding.

Dad handled our mother's hospital admissions, endured her volatile moods, vetted the care options available to her, and supervised her caretaking in several different facilities to make sure that she received the best care possible. He was indefatigable in his unending efforts to brighten what was left of Mom's life, visiting her almost daily, bringing her treats, and decorating her room with pictures and familiar keepsakes aimed at making each new environment as comforting and nonthreatening as possible. In demonstrating his love and concern by so closely attending to her needs, Dad inspired the affection, admiration, and allyship of the caregivers tasked with the difficult job of caring for her, thus ensuring that she always remained in loving hands.

Over the course of the years, all of this added up to a formidable task that for many people would have been a crushing burden, but for our father was a load he carried with uncommon grace, almost single-handedly and without complaint.

Although we dearly miss our mother's wit and wisdom and grieve with our father for the loss of the deep and lasting bond they shared, we feel so very blessed that our amazing dad is still with us. He has persevered through so much to honor Mom's memory and pass along the fruits of his hard-won experience in an attempt to help others, hopefully including the readers of this book. We salute you, Dad, and offer you our heartfelt thanks.

With love and gratitude,
Martha L. Hansen and Ellen H. Dunham

ABOUT THE AUTHOR

W. LEE HANSEN, University of Wisconsin-Madison professor emeritus, economics, earned undergraduate and master's degrees at UW-Madison (1950, 1955), and a Ph.D. in political economy from Johns Hopkins University (1958). He taught at UCLA, held a postdoctoral fellowship at the University of Chicago, was a senior staff economist for the President's Council of Economic Advisers, and had visiting appointments at the London School of Economics, the University of Sydney, the University of Western Australia, and Maastricht University. He became professor emeritus in 1998. His numerous awards include a Distinguished Teaching Award and the Hilldale Award for Distinguished Professional Achievement at UW-Madison.

He has had a longtime interest in academic freedom, due process, and faculty governance. He is a member of AAUP and also UW-Madison's independent Committee on Academic Freedom and Rights that brought about the end of the UW-Madison faculty speech code in 2009. He is editor of the book *Academic Freedom on "Trial": 100 Years of Sifting and Winnowing at the University of Wisconsin* (1998). Since the mid-1990s he has been writing about "diversity" as it is practiced at UW-Madison.

ACKNOWLEDGMENTS

I OWE THANKS TO several groups of talented, caring individuals, some of whom cared for Sally during her long siege of dementia, others who assisted me in writing this story about the institutional care she received, and finally those who helped design and publish this book. Plus a number of personal friends who provided emotional support as I worked my way thought Sally's final years, among them Dick Goldberg and Lisa Munro, and Brian Joiner and Lynnie Clemens, my two historian friends at Oakwood Bob Frykenberg and Stanley Paine, the dozen members of my more than 28 year-old ABC book discussion group, and an editor, Sharon Van Sluijs, who assisted me on two other on-going writing projects. I thank Nina Goldberg for giving me permission to reprint the poem "Untitled" by her mother Iefke Goldberger.

I begin by thanking Sally's primary care doctors at Associated Physicians and UW Hospital, and the several psychiatrists for the care they provided Sally during her almost fifty years living in Madison and especially during the first seven years of Sally's dementia, the succession of caregivers who took over at Oakwood Village, beginning with those in Tabor Assisted Living, followed by those in Covenant Memory Care, and then by those in Hebron Skilled Nursing Care. The Shorewood Hills EMS crews and the City of Madison's EMS crews who responded so quickly, effectively, and so often in transporting Sally to the UW Hospital Emergency Room, followed by UW Hospital doctors and staff in the Geriatric and General wards, the accomplished staff of doctors, nurses, certified nursing staff, and volunteers who make Agrace Hospice such a wonderful caring refuge where so many people can obtain long-term care while the terminally ill can spend their final days and die with dignity. And then there is Madison's BrightStar Senior

Living community with its experienced Wellness Nurse, Robyn Shearer, ts Executive Director Bonnie Banker, and its home care director Wendy Sulzer who made the final eighteen months of Sally's Memory and End-of-Life Care the best one could ever hope for. Literally hundreds of health professions have been involved in Sally's care, and all of them performed with skill and compassion for this poor woman whose hope was to experience as quickly as possible a peaceful, painless death.

I also thank the many individuals who convinced me that I should write the story of Sally's dementia and eventual death and highlight her strongly held belief in an individual's Right to Die. Principal among them are Julie Leary, then Director of the UW-Madison Writer Institute, who got me started on a first draft, Julie Tallard Johnson, Judith Leary's colleague, who pushed me to complete my first draft and improve the organization and content of the manuscript, the late Anne Dillon a talented freelance editor who contributed greatly to the improvement of my prose while at the same time suggesting what needed to be pruned from the manuscript and what needed to be reorganized to make the manuscript more readable and more attractive to potential readers. Several local writers, Jean Lind, Karen Holden, and Jan Coombs offered excellent advice I was happy to receive; Jan especially who pushed me to tell the "story" of Sally's passage through her ever worsening stages of dementia. My two brothers were most supportive, one whose wife died of dementia a year before sally, and who how at age 90 is living with dementia. Several talks on the subject proved useful in sharpening the focus of my manuscript. My two daughters gave final approval to what I say about their Mother and her suffering, as well as what I write about their suffering. My thanks go out to everyone mentioned above.

I thank my writing mentor Julie Talllard Johnson for her diligence in keeping me on track in bringing this manuscript to completion. I also thank her for putting me in touch with Kristin Mitchell of Little Creek Press for the book design, managing the production process, and invaluable advice. I thank Heidi Overson whos careful editing and proofing saved me from much embarrassment.

Printed in the United States
by Baker & Taylor Publisher Services